NATIONAL STANDARDS
& BEST PRACTICES
for U.S. MUSEUMS

The American Association of Museums
Commentary by Elizabeth E. Merritt

AMERICAN ASSOCIATION OF MUSEUMS

© 2008 American Association of Museums
1575 Eye Street, N.W.
Washington, DC 20005

© 2008 American Association of Museums, 1575 Eye St., N.W., Suite 400, Washington, DC 20005; www.aam-us.org. This publication may not be reproduced, in whole or in part, in any form, except for brief passages by reviewers, without written permission from the publisher.

John Strand, Publisher
Lisa Meyerowitz, Associate Editor
Susan v. Levine, Art Director
Kirsten Ankers, Designer

Library of Congress Cataloging-in-Publication Data
American Association of Museums.
  National standards and best practices for U.S. museums / by the American Association of Museums ; with commentary by Elizabeth E. Merritt.
      p. cm.
   ISBN 978-1-933253-11-4 (alk. paper)
   1. Museums--United States--Handbooks, manuals, etc. 2. Museums--Standards--United States--Handbooks, manuals, etc. 3. Museum techniques--United States--Handbooks, manuals, etc. 4. Museums--United States--Management--Handbooks, manuals, etc. I. Merritt, Elizabeth E. II. Title.
   AM11.A63 2008
   069'.068--dc22
                              2008010792

NATIONAL STANDARDS
& BEST PRACTICES
for U.S. MUSEUMS

CONTENTS

PREFACE

What makes for a great museum? We're all sure we know one when we see it. But if you went to a given institution and asked a trustee, an assistant curator, the director, a guy in marketing and a few randomly selected visitors some basic questions—what the museum's goals are, how well it's accomplishing them, what its goals should be—you might find that nobody agrees on what everybody knows.

Hence, this book. One of AAM's key roles is to provide the museum community with forums for discussion, education and exchange, from our annual meeting to our professional education seminars to publications like this one. *National Standards and Best Practices for U.S. Museums* synthesizes the experience and best thinking of leading professionals, looking both inward at how museums function and outward toward their role in society at large. Our goal: to offer specific ways to think more deeply about making your institution the best it can be and provide tools to bring your ideas to fruition.

Ford W. Bell, DVM
President
American Association of Museums

ACKNOWLEDGMENTS

It is my privilege to write the commentary for the first print edition of *National Standards and Best Practices for U.S. Museums*. As part of my work at the American Association of Museums (AAM), I help the board of directors corral the widely dispersed standards and best practices documents that have accumulated over several decades, and herd them into a coherent whole. For many years the AAM Code of Ethics for Museums, standards in the Accreditation Program and other AAM statements have guided the behavior of museums in the U.S. Not until 2006 (fortuitously, AAM's centennial), however, did the board formally designate these as national standards for the field. This process is ongoing, as AAM ushers the standards and best practices developed through the 13 AAM Standing Professional Committees into this assemblage. And new standards will be written in the coming years to meet changing expectations and emerging challenges.

The standards and best practices are presented in Section 2. In the accompanying text, I provide context, drawing on my experiences in the museum field for more than twenty-three years, the last eight at AAM, where I work closely with the Accreditation and Museum Assessment Programs, and the ethics task force of the AAM board. In my position, I spend a lot of time talking with people about how museums should and do behave. If a museum director is upset about an accreditation decision, they call. If the press contacts AAM asking whether a museum has violated museum standards, media relations staff talk to me about it. When the Accreditation Commission wrestles over appropriate standards and how they should be applied, I listen and push them to dig deep into the hard questions.

I have summarized my observations of the real-life situations in which the standards are tested, how museums put them into practice and where the biggest problems are likely to arise. Much of it is drawn, practically verbatim, from conversations I have had over and over again with museum professionals across the country. In other words, this has been road-tested by your peers. I hope you find it to be useful to you, as well.

The commentary in this book reflects the collective wisdom of many, many people in the museum field. Any original contributions I have made are based on what I have learned from them. Chief among these are the members of the Accreditation Commission, who devote hundreds of hours each year to reading about and discussing museums under their review. I am particularly grateful to the past and current chairs of the commission, Marty Sullivan, director of Historic St. Mary's City, and Jim Welu, director of the Worcester Art Museum. Their patient tutelage, as we worked through hard decisions, has been an unparalleled education.

I thank my colleagues Eileen Goldspiel, Julie Hart, Kim Igoe, Erik Ledbetter and Helen Wechsler, whose deep understanding in the realms of accreditation standards, national and international museum ethics, government regulation and journalism has contributed enormously to the detail and accuracy of the information in this book. Any errors or omissions, should something have evaded their eagle eyes, are due to this author. I owe a particular debt to Victoria Garvin, who, when starting her job as AAM's first standards research/writer almost a decade ago, first raised the question, "So where are the standards, anyway?" (At that time, AAM had not officially approved any!) While she has moved on to other challenges, in writing this book, I frequently heard Victoria's voice in my head critiquing the text, pushing me to be clear and precise in my explanations.

I have learned that nothing cultivates good writing like good editing, and I thank John Strand and Lisa Meyerowitz for gently shepherding an initially sprawling manuscript to coherence. I am a better writer and thinker for their mentoring. My thanks to Kirsten Ankers and Susan v. Levine for their design expertise, adding beauty to truth.

I am grateful to my husband, Cliff Duke, for his patient listening on the frequent mornings that I felt the need to dissect the coverage in the *New York Times* regarding museums and their (mis)behavior. Lastly, *spasibo* to my fencing coach, Vitali Pokalenko, for continually reminding me not to be so serious. I hope, in this text, I have followed his advice.

Elizabeth E. Merritt
Founding Director, Center for the Future of Museums

SECTION 1
INTRODUCTION

Who Should Use this Book and How

This book provides an overview of national museum standards (things all good museums should do) and best practices (commendable actions for which they should get extra credit). It explains how the standards are developed, who uses them and for what purposes, and how your museum can use them to guide operations. By presenting standards and best practices in one place, together with a common-sense exploration of what they look like in application, this book lays the groundwork for any serious discussion of what a museum can or should do. So share it widely with people with whom these discussions take place. You may want to give copies to:

- *members of your governing authority*: to help them understand the standards guiding the decisions of the staff, and by which their performance as board members will be judged by the outside world;
- *staff*: to establish a common culture and a sound basis for developing museum policies and procedures;
- *people engaged in creating your institutional plan*: so that attainment of museum standards guides your long-term goals;
- *administrators in your parent organization (if you have one) such as a college, municipality, for-profit company or foundation*: to foster an environment in which the museum can flourish and administrators can help to achieve museums' goals;
- *journalists*: to inform the way they write about your museum and better equip them to educate the public about museums in general;
- *funders and granting agencies*: so that they know that you know the standards and to help them establish appropriate criteria for deciding whether your museum is deserving of support.

Section 2 presents the standards themselves, first the overarching Characteristics of Excellence, then each of seven areas of performance addressed by the Characteristics. Each of these seven sections restates the Characteristics related to this area of performance; presents more detailed standards related to this area; provides commentary on issues that frequently cause problems or provoke questions; and outlines any related best practices.

What Is a Museum?

A museum is a place which invites, in a special way, to contemplation and musing about our humanly strive after truth, goodness and beauty. This contemplation and musing brighten at one side the notion of our nullity and transitoriness, but reinforce at the other side the experience of our mysterious relationship and linking with the Imperishable.
—F. J. C. J. NUYENS, DUTCH SOCIOLOGIST, 1981

Various attempts have been made over the years to draw firm boundaries around the category "museums," defining who gets in and who stays out. Some things people have tried to take into account are:

▸ Whether the organization is nonprofit (private or governmental) as opposed to for-profit. Left outside in the cold using this criteria are institutions such as the International Spy Museum, the Biltmore Estate, Graceland, the American International Rattlesnake Museum and the Museum of Sex, not to mention numerous very small museums that have not gotten around to being formally incorporated as nonprofits. (For example, the World's Smallest Museum, in Superior, Ariz., which has a total interior space of 134 square feet.) While museum professionals may feel strongly that nonprofit status is an important way to establish that the primary purpose of the majority of museums is serving the public benefit, the average person walking in off the street would recognize any of the institutions mentioned above as fitting his or her concept of a museum.

▸ Whether the organization has education as one of its core functions. Most everyone agrees this is an appropriate criterion, but when you realize that education can encompass almost any form of learning about anything, it becomes so broad as to be useless as a boundary. Would you argue about the educational nature or content of the Museum of Advertising Icons, the Dr. Pepper Museum and Free Enterprise Institute or the Museum of Jurassic Technology? They may not present traditional art, history or science, but they provide fascinating explorations of their topics of choice. And what to make of the Bloedel Reserve of Bainbridge Island, Wash., which identifies its purpose as "to provide people with an opportunity to enjoy nature through quiet walks in the gardens and woodlands"? It is undoubtedly a public garden, and hence a museum, but as education goes, it doesn't get much more low-key than that. And, for that matter, how does this help distinguish museums from libraries or schools or dance studios or other types of organizations that are clearly educational in nature?

▸ The care, preservation and display of objects. Historically, this may have been true, but the late twentieth century saw the proliferation of organizations broadly recognized as museums that do not care for, own or use collections—for example, many children's museums and science centers use objects as props but do not regard them as collections held in the public trust. Currently, 10 percent of museums identify themselves as not owning or using collections.[1]

▶ Whether the organization has a physical location (which may itself be a historic artifact) and delivers much of its interpretive content through experiences at that location. A growing number of museums, however, are virtual, existing only on the Internet. They may be grounded in a physical location with collections that are not open to the public, but for some there is no "there" there. They are completely virtual organizations of knowledge and images with no physical presence (other than the server on which the site is housed). (See, for example, the International Spaceflight Museum, which is "located" in the Internet-based virtual world Second Life.) Even traditional site-based museums serve a growing number of people through their websites—their site visitation far surpassing their physical visitors. If the physical site closed or went away but the website remained, would it be any less a museum?

We may have to live with the fact that "museum" as a concept is the intersection of many complex categories, resulting in an organization that people can identify intuitively but that cannot be neatly packaged in a definition.

Where does this leave us in creating standards for this ill-defined bunch? The American Association of Museums takes a "big tent" approach. If an organization considers itself to be a museum, it's in the tent. This means the universe of American museums, from our point of view, includes the small cadre of for-profit museums, together with the vast majority of nonprofit; non–collections-based museums as well as the traditional collecting institutions; organizations that care for living collections (zoos, botanic gardens, aquariums); as well as the museums of art, history and science. Our intuitive judgment that this apparently diverse group belongs together is born out by the fact that they can, in fact, agree on standards that apply to all of them.

Why Standards?

Standard: something used as a measure, norm or model in comparative evaluations; a required or agreed level of quality or attainment.

—COMPACT OXFORD ENGLISH DICTIONARY

It is human nature to compare ourselves to others—we want to know that we are doing the right thing, and we want to know how we measure up. With personal conduct, we compare ourselves against cultural norms—unwritten rules of conduct, ethics, morality; and societal benchmarks—such as IQ tests, educational degrees, performance evaluations, salaries. Judging by popular magazines, Americans are irresistibly drawn to self-scored "How Am I Doing?" quizzes for everything from dating, appearance and sexual performance to achievement of life goals.

It is only natural that we carry this over into our jobs. Each specialized endeavor, from the moment it is founded, starts creating its own specialized points of comparison. For individuals, what does it mean to be a good mechanic, a good doctor or a good psychic? For organizations, what does it mean to be a good university, a good veterinary clinic or a good organic farm? In some ways these organizations have it easy. If they ask to be judged by outcomes, their effects are easy to describe: students who pass exams and get jobs; pets that are cured or comforted at the end of life; produce that is chemical-free. Museums have a harder time defining, as a field, the effect we are trying to produce, at least in any way that is clear and measurable. As providers of informal learning experiences, we may or may not be able to track and measure the effect we have on what people know or think. And the knowledge we provide is not always a concrete fact or way of thinking. Often it is an experience—the sum total of sights and sounds and smells, tactile impressions, emotions—that adds to the life experience that shapes who we are.

Yet the vast majority of museums in the U.S. are nonprofit and ask for public support in one form or another in return for providing some kind of public good. So it is important that we be broadly accountable for our conduct, not just to the users of our services but to society as a whole. While some individual museums measure and report the effect they have on their audience and communities, such practice is rare, and field-wide studies are scarcer still. That makes it all the more important that we have clearly agreed-upon standards that describe what it means to be a "good" museum, one worthy of public support and trust.

Also, as we are responsible for administering somewhere between $4.5 billion and $6 billion in government and private support, museums are understandably a subject of scrutiny by regulators.[2] Adherence to mutually agreed-upon standards enables museums to self-regulate, to a large extent, in a flexible and appropriate way that accommodates the huge diversity of our field. When standards are poorly articulated in an important area of operations, or a museum's conduct seems to contravene generally accepted (if unwritten) public standards, the government steps in, and we get federal or state or local laws and regulations that may or may not be sensible and applicable to museums of all types and sizes.

Last but not least, museums are closely watched by the some 67,000 members of the American media—self-appointed guardians of the public interest and government oversight. Journalists are society's watchdogs, and while we might not like it when we are at the receiving end of their scrutiny, their zealous attention to museum behavior (and museum misbehavior does make for great headlines) keeps us appropriately on our toes. They constantly test whether we are able to credibly explain our actions and justify to the general public why they are reasonable and appropriate in the context of our self-identified standards.

SOME CHARACTERISTICS OF STANDARDS

Standards reflect areas of broad agreement. If people have not come to consensus, or pretty close, there can't be a standard, because nothing has been generally agreed upon. That means there may be very important areas of conduct for which there are no standards, as museums try out different types of behavior, see how their colleagues, the general public, regulators and the media react to these experiments, and adjust their actions accordingly. Sometimes these discussions can go on for decades without a consensus.

Standards reflect areas where things actually go wrong. People don't write standards about behavior that doesn't happen. A situation recently arose in which the Los Angeles Museum of Contemporary Art included a Louis Vuitton boutique in the middle of its exhibition on the Japanese artist Takashi Murakami. Murakami is known for exploring the fuzzy boundaries between art and commerce, particularly his collaboration with Vuitton. The profits from the boutique went to the Vuitton company, not the museum. Some people started questioning whether this is ethical. Does it contravene standards? Well, no. At this moment the standards don't say anything about having a for-profit company running a store in the middle of an exhibit. As far as I know, no museum ever tried it before, so the issue hasn't come up and the broader ethical issue has not been debated.

Standards change over time. Museum standards arise out of technical knowledge (how to do things well, like conservation or education) and out of attitudes regarding what is right and appropriate (ethics). Both technical knowledge and attitudes evolve over time. As we come to appreciate the complexities of the effects of RH and temperature on objects and buildings, our technical standards for climate control become more and more nuanced. I remember when the rule handed down from on high regarding climate control was "55 percent humidity, +/- 3 percent." End of story. Now we recognize that you can't expect a museum housed in a brick building in Bishop, Calif. (average relative humidity 20 percent) to maintain an interior relative humidity of 55 percent— the brick would spall. Society changes, too, and museum standards evolve within this larger cultural environment. Fifty years ago it was simply accepted that museums owned human remains and sacred objects from other cultures. Now there is considerable debate about whether and when this is ethical. And because museums lagged behind societal expectations in this regard, failing to develop and apply credible self-imposed standards, Congress passed the Native American Graves Protection and Repatriation Act (NAGPRA), legislating how museums must deal with federally recognized tribes and Native Hawaiian organizations. NAGPRA has worked out pretty well, but maybe if museums had voluntarily worked with tribal representatives to develop a mutually acceptable solution, it would have been even better in terms of efficiency and effectiveness (two characteristics not usually attributed to government regulations). Implementation also might have been easier, starting from a premise of trust and goodwill.

Consequently, this book is a snapshot of a rapidly changing landscape. While you use it, pay attention to what may happen in the next week, month or year by reading professional publications, attending local, state and regional museum meetings, checking the websites of AAM and other museum professional associations, and talking to colleagues.

Standards come from broad dialogue. To be appropriate and credible, standards need to be created through a process that incorporates input of people in institutions expected to abide by the standards and of people who hold those expectations. For this reason it is important that you be an active participant in the ongoing discussion that culminates in written standards—to be appropriate for all museums, standards need input from professionals at museums of all types and sizes. Given the increasing pressure for public accountability, we also need input from members of the public, policymakers and media who use these standards to assess whether museums live up to their expectations. You can help by educating your museum's funders, local policymakers and media, and national representatives about museum standards, drawing them into this discussion, as well.

What Are "Standards and Best Practices"?

If it is hard to pin down one thing that identifies a museum, it is easy to characterize people who work in museums: We love to argue about the meaning of words. This book could be ten times as long and only begin to cover the debate that ensues from an open discussion of the definition of *standard*. To forestall that debate (and move quickly to the important business of determining what the standards actually are), the AAM Board of Directors approved the following definitions. Of course, we can't make the rest of the field adopt these definitions universally, but at least it establishes what they mean for the purposes of understanding the material in this book.

> *Standards* are generally accepted levels of attainment that all museums are expected to achieve. *Best practices* are commendable actions and philosophies that demonstrate an awareness of standards, successfully solve problems, can be replicated and that museums may choose to emulate if appropriate to their circumstances.

Translated into plain English: Standards are things that all good museums should live up to, and they can expect to be criticized by colleagues, or supporters or the press, if they don't. Standards are not lofty goals that only a few will achieve they are fundamental to being a good museum, a responsible nonprofit and a well-run business. Best practices are "extra credit." Museums deserve applause if they can implement them but shouldn't be faulted if they can't. Some best practices may not be suitable to a museum's particular circumstances, and some museums might not have the resources needed to go that extra mile.

Where Do Standards Come From?

There are more than 17,000 museums in the U.S., with more than 200,000 employees.[3] These museums range in size from all-volunteer to more than 300 paid staff. Their annual operating expenses can be counted in the hundreds of dollars or in the high millions. They include historic sites and houses, zoos, art museums, history museums, science centers, children's museums, nature centers and botanic gardens (to name but a few). It is truly daunting to imagine inventing a system to establish standards appropriate for all of these organizations.

Fortunately, the museum field did not have to create this system all at once—it evolved on its own, through almost four decades of experimentation. And the method, in concept, is very simple: Get enough people representing these diverse museums talking to each other, give them ways to look closely at a lot of different museums and how they operate, share observations about what works and what does not work, discuss what is and is not appropriate, write it down, report it to the field, see what gets accepted or shot down and revise accordingly. This takes place through the activities of the several dozen professional associations representing various parts of the museum field, with AAM representing the whole.

Within AAM, this ongoing exploration of standards principally takes place through the Accreditation Program, ethics task forces empanelled by the AAM Board of Directors and the Standing Professional Committees (which represent various segments of the museum profession: curators, registrars, educators, security staff, etc.)

Of these, the Accreditation Program has had the biggest influence in creating written standards for museums. We say more about the Accreditation Program's role in recognizing achievement and enforcing standards on page 11. Here we focus on its role in codifying museum standards. There are about 800 museums in the Accreditation Program (more than 770 accredited, a couple dozen applicants). To earn accreditation they complete a detailed self-study of all areas of their operations. Two peer reviewers (senior staff from comparable institutions) read the self-study, visit the museum and write a report summarizing their observations. Finally the self-study and report are reviewed by nine museum professionals who volunteer to serve on the Accreditation Commission. Based on this information, the commission decides to accredit the museum, to table its decision while asking the museum to make improvements in areas where it falls short of standards, or denies accreditation. There may be considerable follow-up discussion (as you may imagine) between the commission, museum and peer reviewers regarding these decisions.

When the program began in the early 1970s, it was pretty informal. Staff provided some minimal written guidance for the peer reviewers, focusing their attention on certain areas of operations, but there were no written standards per se. As the peer reviewers, the commissioners, and museums whose fates were being decided wrestled with how to make fair and equitable decisions, it became clear that it was necessary to have a set of objective criteria by which museums can be assessed—rules that everyone would know ahead of time so that the commission would have a common point of reference during the deliberations. These rules have evolved and expanded over time, forming the core of what has become *National Standards and Best Practices for U.S. Museums.*

The other document central to national museum standards is the Code of Ethics for Museums, written in 1978, and most recently revised in 2000, which guides museums' creation of their own individualized codes of ethics. This and other ethics statements approved by the AAM board are issued to the field for comment (and lively debate) before being approved. This process may include national colloquiums on a given topic (like those held in 2002 and 2005 on collections planning and interpretive planning, respectively); sessions at professional meetings; formal comment periods; and referral to specific related task forces or committees of other organizations.

This process is mirrored in the various discipline-specific museum associations that create standards applicable to the segment of the museum community that they represent—the American Association for State and Local History, Association of Children's Museums, Association of Science and Technology Centers, etc. Taken together, these written standards create an overlapping web of guidance that apply at the broadest level to all museums, and then drill down to practices or ethics specific to particular fields.

In sum, museum standards arise from a big, messy dialogue that corrals all this input into a form approved by the field as a whole, as represented by staff who are actively engaged in the work of their professional associations. In this way, we ensure that the standards are applicable to, appropriate for and achievable by all types of museums.

How Can Museums Use the Standards?

The board, staff and volunteers who govern and operate museums come from diverse backgrounds, cultures and training. Staff may be trained in museum studies programs, where they learn how nonprofits work in general, or they may come from specialized academic programs about their subject (art, science, history) and have little or no knowledge of the legal and ethical underpinnings of nonprofit operations. Some people primarily learn on the job, but practices vary from museum to museum. And particularly in small or isolated institutions, norms can drift away from those of the field as a whole. Some staff, many board members and volunteers—and with increasing frequency, the director—come from the for-profit world and bring an entirely different set of assumptions about what is right and appropriate behavior for the organization or its employees. Museums that exist inside non-museum entities (for instance, universities or city or state governments) may report to individuals whose instinct is to apply the conventions of the bigger entity to the museum, regardless of whether this would conflict with usual museum practice.

Many of the conflicts that arise in the course of running a museum happen in part because people assume they are all speaking the same language. In fact, nonprofits in general and museums specifically have a very detailed and arcane language that guides their thinking. Ensuring that all parties engaged in leading and operating the museum understand museum standards provides the beginning of a common vocabulary. As noted in *Getting to Yes,* a classic 1981 text on difficult negotiations, having objective criteria for decision making can help parties with disparate needs arrive at wise and efficient solutions. People usually can agree that nationally approved standards are an appropriate set of measures to guide their discussions.

Here are some opportunities to expose people to the standards in order to help build a shared culture:

▶ *When people are hired, elected to the board or recruited as volunteers*: Include a copy of the "Characteristics of Excellence for U.S. Museums" in your personnel policy, board briefing book, volunteer manual or the equivalent. Present an overview of the standards in orientation sessions for staff, board members and volunteers.

▶ *When the museum is engaged in planning*: Museum standards should inform the goals the museum sets in its planning process. Some museums make meeting standards, or gaining recognition for meeting standards through becoming accredited, a goal in and of itself. When the planning team begins to meet, include the standards with the other basic documents the team might review as it begins its work (e.g., the last plan, the museum's recent financial statement, feasibility studies, etc.).

▶ *When staff and board write policies*: The first thing a museum's conduct will be judged by is whether it is in alignment with the museum's own policies. These, in turn, should be consistent with all the applicable national and discipline-specific standards. While an individual may not like a museum's actions, it is hard to make a case for those actions being objectively "wrong" if they are in accord with policies established in advance by people acting in good faith, and ratified by the opinion of their colleagues. It is, of course, crucial that these policies have been established *before* the action took place. (There is nothing like after-the-fact ratification to make an otherwise innocent action smell like a dead fish.) It is also important that they be publicly available—showing that the museum feels they will stand up to public scrutiny.

▶ *When the museum asks for support*: It benefits individual museums and the field as a whole when private donors, foundations, grant-making agencies and policymakers understand what constitutes a "good" museum worthy of their support. When you cultivate donors, write grant proposals and work with your local, state or national political representatives, integrate information on the standards and how you meet them into your message.

▶ *When you make any important decision, and when you prepare the accompanying communications plan*: Will you be able to explain how the museum's actions are in line with national standards? As discussed in Section 3, often when a museum lands in the news for something the press or public regard as questionable, they call AAM and we refer them to the national standards to guide their assessment of the museum's actions. So test your decision against the standards before the fact.

▶ *When you assess and report on the museum's performance*: Museums are increasingly called upon to publicly account for what they do to deserve public support. While the most meaningful measures document how the museum delivers its mission (the good it does for its community and audience), showing that you comply with national museum standards is a powerful tool for demonstrating to the public, press, policymakers and funders that you make responsible use of the support they provide. Museums can measure and report on this themselves, engage outside consultants, participate in peer-based programs such as the Museum Assessment and Conservation Assessment Programs or receive outside certification of meeting standards by becoming accredited.

Who Else Uses the Standards, and How?

Increasingly, funders use nationally recognized criteria for assessing whether museums deserve support. Some take into account whether a museum is accredited—accepting this third-party certification that the organization meets national standards. Florida, for example, requires museums to be accredited to receive some kinds of state funding. The Kresge Foundation and other major funders consider accredited status when reviewing grant proposals. The Institute of Museum and Library Services weighs a museum's participation in the Museum Assessment Program and the priorities it establishes through peer review against standards in that program in awarding competitive Museums for America grants. We do not track how often local and regional funders use such criteria, but we know that there is trend to do so and it is likely to become more common in the future.

Policymakers look to museum standards in deciding whether and how to create legislation or regulations to govern museum behavior. Often the museum field tackles the creation of standards because of a contentious issue in order to forestall government regulation. AAM Guidelines on Individual Donor Support, for example, were written in the wake of the "Sensations" exhibition at the Brooklyn Museum of Art in 1999, which raised issues of whether the lender of the works in the show, Charles Saatchi, exercised undue influence over the content and presentation, and the museum's lack of transparency regarding his support and the extent of his involvement. The state of New York takes accreditation into account when considering whether to charter museums as state nonprofits. Attorneys General in all states consult national standards in weighing the conduct of the nonprofit museums under their oversight. When the AGs do step in to intervene on behalf of the public, either because the museum proactively asks them to or because there is a potential breach of the public trust (such as when the Museum of the City of New York proposed large-scale deaccessioning of its collections), they often take into account ethics and museum standards as well as the law in issuing their decisions and providing guidance to the museum.

Members of the media use museum standards to inform their coverage, particularly regarding controversial actions that some people perceive to be unethical or simply objectionable. AAM is frequently contacted by members of the press about this or that museum, asking whether its behavior aligns with national standards. We don't comment on the actions of individual museums, but we are happy to take the opportunity to educate journalists on museum standards and help them understand how to apply them to their coverage. The topics that most often attract the attention of the press are: deaccessioning, care of collections, executive compensation, financial distress (particularly if it may be a result of financial mismanagement), relationships with individual and corporate donors and conflict of interest.

Members of the public increasingly refer to the standards, as well, particularly if they are irritated by something the museum has done and want to bring it to the attention of the press. It used to be that specialized standards were relatively inaccessible to the general public unless someone was pretty serious about doing research through a library or writing to a professional association. The World Wide Web has made this material easily available to anyone with a browser and some knowledge of how to search the Internet. Museums need to understand that members of their communities and audiences have access to this information—and take this into account when they make decisions and explain them to the public.

MUSEUM ACCREDITATION

In the U.S., compliance with museum standards is voluntary. The pressure brought to bear by funders, regulators, the press and the public may be considerable, but in the end, museums choose to follow or not follow standards of the field.

There is a cadre of museums, however, that have pledged to abide by the standards in a formally certified manner through the AAM Accreditation Program. For the past decade, the number of accredited museums has remained pretty constant, between 750 and 770—about 5 percent of museums in the U.S. We should commend these museums for their commitment to public accountability. By opening up their operations to intense scrutiny by their peers, they burnish the reputation of all museums. They also play a key role in the development of the standards themselves—accreditation being a crucible in which important issues are examined, patterns of behavior are observed to be consistently successful or unsuccessful, and emerging standards are tested for consistency, applicability and appropriateness.

The Accreditation Program constantly changes with time and is undergoing significant revisions even as I write. The broad outline has remained, however, and likely will continue to remain the same since its inception in the early 1970s. In the program, museums:

▶ undertake an intensive self-study, documenting various aspects of their operations. This self-study includes assembling fundamental documents such as plans and policies approved by the governing authority;

▶ open themselves to examination by a committee of their peers, who review the self-study and attached documentation, as well as visit the museum and interview members of the board, staff and volunteers;

▶ are assessed by the Accreditation Commission, composed of museum professionals who volunteer their time to review the self-study, documentation and peer reviewers' report in order to determine whether the museum meets AAM standards.

AAM's website (www.aam-us.org) provides information on how these standards are applied in accreditation and what documents accredited museums must have to demonstrate they are meeting the standards.

In my estimation, from talking with museum staff over the years, for every one museum that has attained accreditation, another ten consciously use museum standards to guide their planning and operations. Some of these museums intend to become accredited eventually. Others feel that while the standards are appropriate and worthy of their attention, they don't need or want the certification per se. And there are a few museums that consciously opt out, deciding, for example, that their institutional culture is not compatible with some of the standards.

There is increasing pressure, however, from policymakers and funders for all non-profits—museums included—to adhere to formal, widely accepted standards and to demonstrate that they are doing so. Given that this trend is likely to continue, museum accreditation—or certification in some way, shape or form—is likely to play a greater role in the future. In this context, the standards set forth in this book, and the methods that museums use to demonstrate that they adhere to these standards, assume an even greater importance. It is in the best interests of museums that the field determines the standards, and the processes by which they will be judged, rather than being subjected to standards or to reporting requirements that do not fit the quirky reality of our nature.

1. Elizabeth E. Merritt, ed., *2006 Museum Financial Information* (Washington, D.C.: American Association of Museums, 2006).

2. Estimated from data gathered through the Museum Financial Information Survey 2005 and U.S. Census Bureau data on employer institutions.

3. Institute for Museum and Library Services estimates that there are 17,500 museums in the U.S., see www.IMLS.gov; employee estimate from AAM analysis of the 2000 Census, accessed through the Missouri Census Data Center http://mcdc2.missouri.edu/.

SECTION 2
STANDARDS AND BEST PRACTICES

Core Questions

Two core questions underlie any assessment of a museum against museum standards: How well does the museum achieve its stated mission and goals? How well does the museum's performance meet standards and best practices, as generally understood in the field and as appropriate to its circumstances?

Commentary

These questions are crucial to the flexible and appropriate application of national standards to museums of all sizes and types.

MISSION AND GOALS

Nonprofit museums exist to serve the public, and a museum explains whom it will serve and how in its mission statement. (See more about mission statements on page 34.) Therefore the principle question guiding any assessment of a museum, whether by the public, media, funders, accreditation reviewers or others, is whether it is successfully meeting this mission. Since a museum has selected its own mission, it has chosen for itself the principle benchmark by which it will be evaluated.

Two museums, essentially identical in their operations but having dissimilar missions, might measure up very differently in light of this principle. A small historic house museum that meets its mission of serving its local community through interpreting neighborhood history might be doing a fine job. Its clone in another city, with equivalent exhibits and programs but an ambitious mission of being a world-class museum advancing scholarship in the field of history, might be found to fall far short of its aspirations.

Mission statements are typically very broad, and most museums could meet their missions in many different ways. Each museum makes more specific choices through its plans, principally the institutional plan (see page 36). These plans establish specific goals, such as "open a new, state-of-the art exhibition wing in three years," "attain museum accreditation" or "double the number of schoolchildren served through programs." The museum's goals, as established in its plans, become important, self-identified indicators of whether the museum is meeting its mission.

"AS APPROPRIATE TO ITS CIRCUMSTANCES"

Clearly a rural arts center, primarily run by volunteers with annual operating expenses of $50,000, is not going to look in any way, shape or form like the Metropolitan Museum of Art. Yet both could be meeting national museum standards. How can this be? It is because they each make intelligent use of available resources to do their work in a way their peers will recognize, in context, as being appropriate to their circumstances. The small arts center might have a 400-square-foot storage room, with art racks made of galvanized pipe, equipped with a hand-filled humidifier for the winter and a dehumidifier (also emptied by hand) for the summer. Copies to the key for the sturdy lock on the door are held by the part-time director and the volunteer curator. Exhibit labels are neatly printed using a Laserjet printer, mounted on foamcore and stuck to the wall with double-sided tape. Most of the lighting is incandescent, and the few fluorescent lights have filters to screen art from harmful ultraviolet wavelengths. The museum's education programs are excellent, taught by a dedicated group of volunteers, each of whom has completed a home study course in art history. Each year they hold an open house for the community, featuring a barbeque in the parking lot and including the local fire and police personnel. Their board of trustees includes representatives of the rapidly growing immigrant communities in their region. What's not to like?

"Appropriate to its circumstances" also takes into account geographic location, audience and community values. For most museums, it would be highly irregular to offer deaccessioned material from the collections back to the original donor. Legally, that donor has no more claim to the object than any other member of the public (i.e., none). The museum's principle responsibility—to use its resources in the public interest—is usually best served by the material going to another nonprofit where it will still be publicly available, or by selling on the open market for the best price possible to give the museum more resources to develop and care for the collections. A number of small, community-based museums, however, have decided that, in some circumstances, offering collections back to the original donor is appropriate. How can they tell a donor, they say, that her grandmother's wedding dress has been sold to a collector halfway across the country? Or that the family Bible now will be in the state archives, 400 miles away?

Characteristics of Excellence for U.S. Museums

The following 38 points, grouped under seven categories, were originally drafted by the Accreditation Commission to provide the big picture of national museum standards. This overview is a good starting point for any examination of the national standards and best practices. The more specific statements branch out from here. Each category will be discussed in more detail in the rest of this section.

I. PUBLIC TRUST AND ACCOUNTABILITY

▶ The museum is a good steward of its resources held in the public trust.

▶ The museum identifies the communities it serves and makes appropriate decisions in how it serves them.

▶ Regardless of its self-identified communities, the museum strives to be a good neighbor in its geographic area.

▶ The museum strives to be inclusive and offers opportunities for diverse participation.

▶ The museum asserts its public service role and places education at the center of that role.

▶ The museum demonstrates a commitment to providing the public with physical and intellectual access to the museum and its resources.

▶ The museum is committed to public accountability and is transparent in its mission and its operations.

▶ The museum complies with local, state and federal laws, codes and regulations applicable to its facilities, operations and administration.

II. MISSION AND PLANNING

▶ The museum has a clear understanding of its mission and communicates why it exists and who benefits as a result of its efforts.

▶ All aspects of the museum's operations are integrated and focused on meeting its mission.

▶ The museum's governing authority and staff think and act strategically to acquire, develop and allocate resources to advance the mission of the museum.

▶ The museum engages in ongoing and reflective institutional planning that includes involvement of its audiences and community.

▶ The museum establishes measures of success and uses them to evaluate and adjust its activities.

III. LEADERSHIP AND ORGANIZATIONAL STRUCTURE

▶ The governance, staff and volunteer structures and processes effectively advance the museum's mission.

▶ The governing authority, staff and volunteers have a clear and shared understanding of their roles and responsibilities.

▶ The governing authority, staff and volunteers legally, ethically and effectively carry out their responsibilities.

▶ The composition, qualifications and diversity of the museum's leadership, staff and volunteers enable it to carry out the museum's mission and goals.

▶ There is a clear and formal division of responsibilities between the governing authority and any group that supports the museum, whether separately incorporated or operating within the museum or its parent organization.

IV. COLLECTIONS STEWARDSHIP

▶ The museum owns, exhibits or uses collections that are appropriate to its mission.

▶ The museum legally, ethically and effectively manages, documents, cares for and uses the collections.

▶ The museum's collections-related research is conducted according to appropriate scholarly standards.

▶ The museum strategically plans for the use and development of its collections.

▶ Guided by its mission, the museum provides public access to its collections while ensuring their preservation.

V. EDUCATION AND INTERPRETATION

▶ The museum clearly states its overall educational goals, philosophy and messages and demonstrates that its activities are in alignment with them.

▶ The museum understands the characteristics and needs of its existing and potential audiences and uses this understanding to inform its interpretation.

▶ The museum's interpretive content is based on appropriate research.

▶ Museums conducting primary research do so according to scholarly standards.

▶ The museum uses techniques, technologies and methods appropriate to its educational goals, content, audiences and resources.

▶ The museum presents accurate and appropriate content for each of its audiences.

▶ The museum demonstrates consistent high quality in its interpretive activities.

▶ The museum assesses the effectiveness of its interpretive activities and uses those results to plan and improve its activities.

VI. FINANCIAL STABILITY

▶ The museum legally, ethically and responsibly acquires, manages and allocates its financial resources in a way that advances its mission.

▶ The museum operates in a fiscally responsible manner that promotes its long-term sustainability.

VII. FACILITIES AND RISK MANAGEMENT

▶ The museum allocates its space and uses its facilities to meet the needs of the collections, audience and staff.

▶ The museum has appropriate measures to ensure the safety and security of people, its collections and/or objects and the facilities it owns or uses.

▶ The museum has an effective program for the care and long-term maintenance of its facilities.

▶ The museum is clean, well maintained and provides for the visitors' needs.

▶ The museum takes appropriate measures to protect itself against potential risk and loss.

Each of the preceding 38 bullets represents a huge amount of reflection on the part of all the people involved in developing the standards. Each word was carefully chosen, and the meanings and implications discussed at great length. Still, the overall effect can be daunting. Sometimes people get too hung up on the wording for this very reason—they sense the work that went into them and try to parse every "the," "and" and "so."

To get past this hurdle and help people focus on the intent behind the careful wording, AAM staff have taken the liberty of translating the Characteristics from official language into, well, plain English. This version, while a bit tongue-in-cheek, is actually a very useful way of showing people how commonsensical, achievable and necessary the Characteristics are. You may want to distribute this version when introducing museum standards to a new audience.

The Characteristics of Excellence for U.S. Museums "in Translation"

I. PUBLIC TRUST AND ACCOUNTABILITY

Accountability

- Be good.
- No really—not only be legal, but be ethical.
- Show everyone how good and ethical you are (don't wait for them to ask).

Community engagement

- Do good for people.
- Know which people.
- And to be on the safe side:
  - Be nice to everyone else, too . . .
  - Especially if they live next door.

Diversity and inclusiveness

- Avoid cloning your staff or board members.
- Look something like the people you are doing good for . . .
- And maybe a bit like your neighbors.
- Let other people help decide what games to play . . .
- And what the rules are.
- Share your toys.

II. MISSION AND PLANNING

Misson

▶ Know what you want to do . .

▶ And why it makes a difference to anyone.

▶ Then put it in writing.

▶ Stick to it.

Planning

▶ Decide what you want to do next.

▶ When you are deciding what to do, ask lots of people for their opinions.

▶ Put it in writing . . .

▶ Then do it.

▶ If it didn't work, don't do it again.

▶ If it did work, do.

III. LEADERSHIP AND ORGANIZATIONAL STRUCTURE

Make sure everyone is clear about who is doing what

▶ The board knows it is governing.

▶ The director knows s/he is directing (and the board knows it, too).

▶ The staff knows it is doing everything else.

▶ And put it in writing.

IV. COLLECTIONS STEWARDSHIP

▶ Know what stuff you have.

▶ Know what stuff you need.

▶ Know where it is.

▶ Take good care of it.

▶ Make sure someone gets some good out of it . . .

▶ Especially people you care about . . .

▶ And your neighbors.

V. EDUCATION AND INTERPRETATION

- Know whom you are talking to.
- Ask them what they want to know.
- Know what you want to say (and what you are talking about).
- Use appropriate language (or images, or music).
- Make sure people understand you.
- And ask them if they like it.
- If not, change it.

VI. FINANCIAL STABILITY

- Put your money where your mission is.
- Is it enough money?
- Will it be there next year, too?
- Know when you will need more money.
- Know where you are going to get it.
- Don't diddle the books.

VII. FACILITIES AND RISK MANAGEMENT

- Don't crowd people . . .
- Or things.
- Make it safe to visit your museum . . .
- Or work there.
- Keep it clean.
- Keep the toilet paper stocked.
- And if all else fails, know where the exit is (and make sure it is clearly marked).

I. Public Trust and Accountability

Commentary

Public trust and accountability is the newest section of the Characteristics, added in 2004. It reflects growing expectations on the part of the public that they be included in the process of deciding what will be done with the support they provide to museums, and of the public and policymakers that museums tell people what they are doing and why. Because these characteristics are so new, it is hard to say exactly what a museum should do to meet them. The following commentary reflects the reasoning and values underlying these standards. In the absence of the "case law," this may help you decide how best to apply them to your museum's operations.

In the big picture, this new section of the Characteristics of Excellence encompasses one of the first standards tackled by the museum field: ethics. Operating in an ethical manner is fundamental to earning the trust and support of the public. The code of ethics for museums as a field, and standards regarding institutional codes of ethics for individual museums, are presented beginning on page 25.

STEWARDSHIP OF RESOURCES

"The museum is a good steward of its resources held in the public trust." You could almost paraphrase Jewish scholar Hillel and declare, "This is the whole standard... the rest is commentary." A steward takes care of something *on behalf of someone else*. For nonprofit museums, that "someone else" is the public, and the museum is accountable to them for how it manages their property. (This is a slightly metaphorical explanation, but grounded in the law—read Marie Malaro's *Legal Primer on Managing Museum Collections* for a detailed explanation of the legal obligations of stewardship.)

This statement is a good, simple touchstone by which to judge any potential decision. Would a reasonable person consider the museum's action to be consistent with good stewardship of collections, funds, the building or anything else it cares for on his or her behalf? For example, is the compensation provided to the director appropriate in proportion to the museum's overall budget? Is the museum doing a credible job of preserving the collections entrusted to its care? Even if you think reasonable people could disagree on the answer to a particular question, framing it in this way can help clarify potential concerns.

COMMUNITIES AND NEIGHBORS

Nonprofit status is granted to museums in recognition of the fact that our organizations provide a public service—in return for public support, we devote our "profits" to creating a better society. But thinking has changed dramatically in the last fifty years about who should benefit as a result of this support. It is not enough anymore to appeal to a small, homogeneous audience (e.g., older white male railroad enthusiasts), and say, "That's who benefits from our work." There is an expectation that any museum serve some broader slice of society.

In particular, there has been a growing consensus in the past couple of decades that museums need to be attentive to the needs of their neighbors—the people who live and work nearby. This may or may not be the same folks the museum has identified as its community of users. Take, for example, a small museum of botany housed in a historic townhouse, in what has become an economically depressed but ethnically diverse neighborhood. The museum preserves and interprets an archive, rare book collection and herbarium. Its mission identifies its audiences as scientists, historians and artists researching the collections. But that museum still affects the people who live around it, even if they never come through its doors. Its physical appearance, the visitors who come into the neighborhood to get to the museum, the accompanying effect on parking, traffic, litter or noise, all influence the quality of life of the museum's neighbors. This standard says that museums have to take these effects into account. The museum might be a good neighbor in ways related to its mission, such as training community gardeners and helping maintain a public green space. Or it might simply make its library, with its Internet-connected computers, available as a quiet, safe place for neighborhood children to do homework in late afternoons.

Happily, as museums put this into practice, they find it is often in their best interests in a business sense, as well. Being involved with your community may lead to your neighbors becoming visitors to your museum. It may build mutually beneficial partnerships with local businesses. It can connect you with people and foundations interested in supporting your museum as much because of your effect on the community as because of belief in your mission (though they may come to care about that, too). It may even inspire a neighborhood kid to grow up to be a botanist, helping with the next challenge on our plate, which is . . .

PUBLIC SERVICE ROLE AND EDUCATION

To be honest, one of the historical reasons that the standards emphasize education as central to the identity of museums is tied to money. Government funding of culture boomed in the 1960s, along with tax reform that forced foundations to give more of their earnings to charity, but this funding was channeled to cultural institutions. At the time, museums were still categorized by the IRS as "recreational," and to qualify for the burgeoning opportunities for tax benefits and grants they needed to position themselves firmly in the educational realm. That said, it is not an inaccurate statement. The history of museums in the U.S. documents their ambitions to educate all classes of society. That is still true today. It is equally true that government, foundations and private funders expect museums to maintain their commitment to filling this role.

DIVERSITY

There is an emerging consensus that museums ought to better reflect the growing diversity of American society in their governance, staffing and audience development. This conversation can quickly bog down in a struggle over what counts when measuring diversity (ethnicity, race, gender, culture, (dis)ability, age, etc.). These issues can't be settled at the national level—the "right" answer is specific to each museum and its circumstances. Clearly a museum in a small agricultural town in rural South Dakota is going to have a harder time recruiting ethnic and cultural diversity than a museum in downtown Chicago. And in any case, for the South Dakota museum, the biggest challenge for board diversity might be finding people under the age of sixty to take the reins.

As with community engagement, the issue is as much practical as it is ideological. According to U.S. Census Bureau projections, by 2050 our population will be "majority minority"—Caucasians of European descent will make up less than 50 percent of the population. If your museum's current audience is primarily composed of the descendants of the founding Europeans, what happens to your institution if only that population cares about your museum? Your base of support will shrink and shrink, and maybe it will become so small the museum is not sustainable. On the other hand, if your story is told in a way that makes it compelling and important to all American citizens, you can make a more diverse audience care about what you do. Or maybe your mission changes over time and addresses broader issues of immigration and celebrates the "founding fathers" (and mothers) of different immigrant groups. In either case, it is difficult for a homogeneous board and staff—however well intentioned—to have "street cred" with groups the museum is trying to reach. People want to see other people like them working in the museum and having a voice in how it is run. And the museum is unlikely to make the best choices about how to serve new audiences without members of those groups helping make the decisions.

ACCESSIBILITY

As all U.S. residents provide support for the museum (through the subsidy of federal or state tax-exempt status, if nothing else, not to mention local bond levies, etc.), everyone should be able to benefit, as far as is practicable, from the museum's assets.

Beyond what is required by law—notably the Americans with Disabilities Act— museums have an ethical imperative to make their resources as accessible as possible. This includes physical assets such as the building and grounds, and intellectual assets—information about the collections, results of the museum's research, exhibits, programs and website.

There may be practical limits to accessibility, often arising from the tension between access and conservation, but museums must do their best to strike an appropriate balance. Unlimited physical access could destroy a museum's ability to preserve its collections, land or historic building for future generations. (And in the case of living animal collections, it could be bad for the preservation of visitors, too.) Unlimited intellectual access might release information in a harmful way. Donors might be put at risk, for example, if museums share information that could lead criminals to target their personal collections. Small populations of threatened or endangered species can be wiped out by commercial dealers or hobbyists if the locations where museum specimens were collected are revealed.

But restricting access is now an exception rather than the rule. Museums are expected to proceed on the assumption that the right to access is a given, and if it is restricted, they should be prepared to answer these questions: What makes this a reasonable restriction? What higher purpose does it serve? No one should have to justify why their group deserves special treatment in order to get into the museum, or be treated with less respect than any other visitor. For example, mobility-impaired visitors should not be relegated to the loading dock or the freight elevator.

ACCOUNTABILITY AND TRANSPARENCY

Gone are the days when museums could say, "Pay no attention to the man behind the curtain." The policies and procedures that guide the museum's operations, its plans for the future and information on how well or poorly it is performing are expected to be made available to anyone who cares enough to look for it. And, increasingly, made available by mail upon written request is not enough. It means making these things a matter of public record—publishing them in newsletters or posting them on the museum's website.

Frankly, most of this information is going to become public one way or another. The website Guidestar (www.guidestar.org) posts electronic copies of all nonprofits' IRS 990 statements, which will only become easier and timelier as the IRS moves toward requiring electronic filing. The IRS itself, aware that many people now use these forms to assess nonprofit performance, is in the midst of redesigning the 990 form to facilitate that kind of analysis. In the world of the Web, any policy or plan, however confidential, can be leaked and posted for the world to see. Far better for the museum to control the medium and the message and take the opportunity to provide context for information that could otherwise be misinterpreted or misunderstood.

LEGAL COMPLIANCE

You might be surprised that legal compliance has to be written into museum standards. But well-meaning individuals often assume their good intentions exempt them from the requirement to follow certain laws and regulations. A children's museum's volunteers may not realize that the kids' group they are running in the morning is, effectively, a daycare center and subject to the relevant codes and regulations. Staff may think that because the museum's closets contain nothing more hazardous than Elmer's glue, acrylic paint, acetone, Lysol, floor wax and drain cleaner, they don't need to provide material safety data sheets to staff and train them how to read them. Even staff of large institutions are vulnerable to this reasoning. Curators returning from field research abroad may think they don't have to declare their animal and plant specimens to Customs, U.S. Fish and Wildlife or U.S. Department of Agriculture personnel because they are scientists—they are doing this for the betterment of mankind, rather than for profit. Ensure that all your staff, board and volunteers are familiar with the relevant laws and regulations governing your museum's actions and know that "this means you."

STANDARDS REGARDING ETHICS
Characteristics of Excellence Related to Ethics

- The museum is a good steward of its resources held in the public trust.
- The museum is committed to public accountability and is transparent in its mission and operations.
- The governing authority, staff and volunteers legally, ethically and effectively carry out their responsibilities.

Commentary

ETHICAL STANDARDS

The following section addresses the two general standards statements regarding ethics: one detailing how each museum creates a tailored code of ethics that governs its actions, the other outlining the general ethical principles to which all U.S. museums subscribe. There are several other standards in this book that one could regard as ethical principles. Some might argue that all big-picture standards, as opposed to technical standards such as what kind of archival ink to use, are about ethics. In any case, these other statements are organized in the sections addressing the areas of operation in question. Section IV: Collections Stewardship addresses loaning collections to non-museum entities and treatment of objects that might have been misappropriated in the Nazi era. Section VI: Financial Stability covers developing and managing business and donor support and retrenchment and downsizing.

The AAM Code of Ethics for Museums

Museums make their unique contribution to the public by collecting, preserving and interpreting the things of this world. Historically, they have owned and used natural objects, living and nonliving, and all manner of human artifacts to advance knowledge and nourish the human spirit. Today, the range of their special interests reflects the scope of human vision. Their missions include collecting and preserving, as well as exhibiting and educating with materials not only owned but also borrowed and fabricated for these ends. Their numbers include both governmental and private museums of anthropology, art history and natural history, aquariums, arboretums, art centers, botanical gardens, children's museums, historic sites, nature centers, planetariums, science and technology centers and zoos. The museum universe in the United States includes both collecting and noncollecting institutions. Although diverse in their missions, they have in common their nonprofit form of organization and a commitment of service to the public. Their collections and/or the objects they borrow or fabricate are the basis for research, exhibits and programs that invite public participation.

Taken as a whole, museum collections and exhibition materials represent the world's natural and cultural common wealth. As stewards of that wealth, museums are compelled to advance an understanding of all natural forms and of the human experience. It is incumbent on museums to be resources for humankind and in all their activities to foster an informed appreciation of the rich and diverse world we have inherited. It is also incumbent upon them to preserve that inheritance for posterity.

Museums in the United States are grounded in the tradition of public service. They are organized as public trusts, holding their collections and information as a benefit for those they were established to serve. Members of their governing authority, employees and volunteers are committed to the interests of these beneficiaries. The law provides the basic framework for museum operations. As nonprofit institutions, museums comply with applicable local, state and federal laws and international conventions, as well as with the specific legal standards governing trust responsibilities. This Code of Ethics for Museums takes that compliance as given. But legal standards are a minimum. Museums and those responsible for them must do more than avoid legal liability, they must take affirmative steps to maintain their integrity so as to warrant public confidence. They must act not only legally but also ethically. This Code of Ethics for Museums, therefore, outlines ethical standards that frequently exceed legal minimums.

Loyalty to the mission of the museum and to the public it serves is the essence of museum work, whether volunteer or paid. Where conflicts of interest arise—actual, potential or perceived—the duty of loyalty must never be compromised. No individual may use his or her position in a museum for personal gain or to benefit another at the expense of the museum, its mission, its reputation and the society it serves.

For museums, public service is paramount. To affirm that ethic and to elaborate its application to their governance, collections and programs, the American Association of Museums promulgates this Code of Ethics for Museums. In subscribing to this code, museums assume responsibility for the actions of members of their governing authority, employees and volunteers in the performance of museum-related duties. Museums, thereby, affirm their chartered purpose, ensure the prudent application of their resources, enhance their effectiveness and maintain public confidence. This collective endeavor strengthens museum work and the contributions of museums to society—present and future.

GOVERNANCE

Museum governance in its various forms is a public trust responsible for the institution's service to society. The governing authority protects and enhances the museum's collections and programs and its physical, human and financial resources. It ensures that all these resources support the museum's mission, respond to the pluralism of society and respect the diversity of the natural and cultural common wealth.

Thus, the governing authority ensures that: all those who work for or on behalf of a museum understand and support its mission and public trust responsibilities; its members understand and fulfill their trusteeship and act corporately, not as individuals; the museum's collections and programs and its physical, human and financial resources are protected, maintained and developed in support of the museum's mission; it is responsive to and represents the interests of society; it maintains the relationship with staff in which shared roles are recognized and separate responsibilities respected; working relationships among trustees, employees and volunteers are based on equity and mutual respect; professional standards and practices inform and guide museum operations; policies are articulated and prudent oversight is practiced; and that governance promotes the public good rather than individual financial gain.

COLLECTIONS

The distinctive character of museum ethics derives from the ownership, care and use of objects, specimens and living collections representing the world's natural and cultural common wealth. This stewardship of collections entails the highest public trust and carries with it the presumption of rightful ownership, permanence, care, documentation, accessibility and responsible disposal.

Thus, the museum ensures that: collections in its custody support its mission and public trust responsibilities; collections in its custody are lawfully held, protected, secure, unencumbered, cared for and preserved; collections in its custody are accounted for and documented; access to the collections and related information is permitted and regulated; acquisition, disposal and loan activities are conducted in a manner that respects the protection and preservation of natural and cultural resources and discourages illicit trade in such materials; acquisition, disposal and loan activities conform to its mission and public trust responsibilities; disposal of collections through sale, trade or research activities occurs solely for the advancement of the museum's mission—proceeds from the sale of nonliving collections are to be used consistently within the established standards of the museum's discipline, but in no event shall they be used for anything other than acquisition or direct care of collections; the unique and special nature of human remains and funerary and sacred objects is recognized as the basis of all decisions concerning such collections; collections-related activities promote the public good rather than individual financial gain; and competing claims of ownership that may be asserted in connection with objects in its custody should be handled openly, seriously, responsively and with respect for the dignity of all parties involved.

PROGRAMS

Museums serve society by advancing an understanding and appreciation of the natural and cultural common wealth through exhibitions, research, scholarship, publications and educational activities. These programs further the museum's mission and are responsive to the concerns, interests and needs of society.

Thus, the museum ensures that: programs support its mission and public trust responsibilities; programs are founded on scholarship and marked by intellectual integrity; programs are accessible and encourage participation of the widest possible audience consistent with its mission and resources; programs respect pluralistic values, traditions and concerns; revenue-producing activities and activities that involve relationships with external entities are compatible with the museum's mission and support its public trust responsibilities; and programs promote the public good rather than individual financial gain.

STANDARDS REGARDING AN INSTITUTIONAL CODE OF ETHICS

All museums are required to have a formally approved, separate and distinct *institutional code of ethics*. An institutional code of ethics should: put forth the institution's basic ethical responsibilities as a *museum and nonprofit educational entity* (not solely be about individual conduct, e.g., conflict of interest issues); be tailored to the museum (it cannot simply be a restatement of the AAM *Code of Ethics for Museums* (2000) or a declaration of adoption of AAM's code, or simply a copy of a parent organization's code); be consistent with the AAM *Code of Ethics for Museums* (2000); state that it applies to members of the governing authority, staff and volunteers; be a single document, not a compilation or list of references to other documents; and be approved by the governing authority.

In addition, the following may be incorporated into the institutional code of ethics, or exist as separate documents, in which case they should be referenced in the institutional code of ethics:

- ▶ Sections on individual ethics, personal conduct and conflict of interest issues that spell out such details for staff, volunteers and members of the governing authority. These sections may exist separately in, for example, a personnel policy.

- ▶ Sections on collections-related ethics. These sections may exist separately in the museum's collections management policies.

- ▶ The museum may also adhere to codes of ethics specific to its discipline/collections (see below) and/or professional museum functions (e.g., *AAM Curators Code of Ethics*). Adoption of these codes cannot replace a separate institutional code. However, if the museum chooses to adhere to these codes, its code of ethics either should incorporate appropriate language from those codes or cite them and indicate that the museum will abide by them.

Museums governed by a larger institution or organization that does not have museum management as its primary operating purpose are required to have an institutional code of ethics that addresses the museum-specific issues outlined in this standard.

PURPOSE AND IMPORTANCE

An institutional code of ethics is important to ensure accountability. The effectiveness of a nonprofit institution is directly related to the public's perception of its integrity. A formally stated institutional code of ethics is evidence of a critical internal process—to write an institutional code of ethics, an institution must collectively discuss the issues it faces and determine what ethical principles are needed to guide its operations and protect its integrity.

It also ensures informed decision making: Developing and implementing an institutional code of ethics leads to informed oversight and benefits the institution in several ways. It creates internal agreement about which actions are consistent with the institution's mission. It serves as a self-made reference point for institutional choices. It also is a practical and effective tool in risk management—protecting both assets and reputation.

An institutional code of ethics expresses the institution's policies, consistent with the public service it affirms in its mission statement. It puts the interests of the public ahead of the interests of the institution or of any individual and encourages conduct that merits public confidence. It acknowledges applicable laws (including the institution's own bylaws or charter) and appropriate discipline-specific professional practices in order to help museums meet or exceed them (see below).

IMPLEMENTATION

A museum's ethical guidelines—either as part of its institutional code or in other approved policies (e.g., personnel policies, collections management policy)—should address: ethical duties of the governing authority, staff and volunteers; ethics related to the relationship of the governing authority and director; conflict of interest (for example: disclosure, gifts and favors, loans, outside employment, personal collecting, purchases of museum property, use of assets, confidentiality); collections ethics issues (for example: acquisition, deaccession, care and preservation/conservation, appraisals, dealing, access to the collection, truth in presentation); museum management practices (for example: legal compliance, ownership of intellectual property/scholarly research, personnel management); and the museum's responsibility to the public. In addition, it is also considered best practice to have policies that address (where applicable): management of business or individual support; commercial activities; and political activities. The institutional code of ethics should also contain a section addressing how the code will be implemented.

EXPECTATIONS TO ABIDE BY DISCIPLINE-SPECIFIC ETHICS STATEMENTS

Museums are expected to abide by "standards and best practices as they are generally understood in the museum field." Some discipline-specific associations have issued ethics statements or guidelines applicable to their disciplines or members. Museums should adhere to these ethics guidelines if they are: broadly applicable to all museums in that segment of the museum field; nonprescriptive—describing desirable outcomes rather than endorsing particular methods of achieving these outcomes; based when possible on applicable existing, widely accepted principles in the field; developed through a broadly inclusive process that gathers input from museums of relevant disciplines, geographic location, size, governance type and other relevant variables.

For example, history organizations are expected to adhere to The Statement of Professional Standards and Ethics of the American Association for State and Local History. Art museums that are members of the Association of Art Museum Directors are expected to adhere to Professional Practices in Art Museums of that association. When developing their codes of ethics, general museums (those that encompass two or more disciplines) must decide how these discipline-specific codes apply to their overall operations and make the reasoning behind those decisions clear.

Commentary

The AAM Code of Ethics and the Standards Regarding an Institutional Code of Ethics, taken together, establish how museums develop ethical guidelines for their institution. The AAM Code of Ethics for Museums outlines the general ethical standards that the field has agreed apply to all museums. It is not, in itself, a code of ethics that can be adopted by a museum—each museum has to write an ethics policy for itself, in alignment with any applicable national standards but tailored to its particular circumstances.

Each museum, in writing its own institutional code of ethics in conformance with the AAM code, expands on it by addressing specific issues, ensuring it fits its circumstances. Engaging the governing authority, staff and volunteers in applying the AAM code to your museum will stimulate the development and maintenance of sound policies and procedures necessary to understanding and ensuring ethical behavior by institutions and all who work for them or on their behalf.

HOW TO TAILOR A CODE OF ETHICS TO YOUR MUSEUM

The most common problem with codes of ethics developed by museums (other than not having one, or simply saying, "We subscribe to the AAM Code of Ethics for Museums") is that many only cover the issues mentioned in the AAM code. But the code talks about issues that may affect all museums, and for which there are standards broadly agreed upon by the field. On many points, the AAM code and other ethics guidelines simple say, "This is important, and each museum has to work out the right answer for itself, guided by the following principles." Some examples of actions (with ethical implications) that a museum might choose to take or not take, or to undertake only in certain ways, and that might be addressed in the museum's institutional code of ethics include: the sale, in the museum store, of work by artists or craftsmen represented in the museum's collection; or of natural history specimens (shells, butterflies, fossils); accepting or not accepting corporate or philanthropic support from particular sources (e.g., tobacco companies, arms manufacturers, the oil industry); disclosure/confidentiality of provenance information such as the identity of donors who wish to remain anonymous, or the collecting locality of rare or endangered species; employment/supervision of a relative of an existing staff or board member; exhibition of collections belonging to or created by staff, a board member or volunteer.

DISCIPLINE-SPECIFIC STANDARDS

It can be challenging to determine whether and when your museum should abide by discipline-specific ethical guidelines. Take the case of a general museum that encompasses art, history and natural history. Should it conform to the AASLH restriction stipulating that funds from the sale of deaccessioned material be used only for acquisition or preservation? (The term, *preservation*, while vague, is still a little more focused than AAM's proviso regarding direct care.) Is this an appropriate restriction to apply to the natural history collections? Or will the museum have different policies for funds resulting from the deaccession and sale of different parts of the collection?

Or, say your institution is an art museum, but not one whose director has been invited to join the limited membership of the Association of Art Museum Directors. Will you abide by standards set by a group that represents only part of your discipline (albeit the largest and most prominent part)?

USE OF FUNDS RESULTING FROM THE SALE OF MATERIAL DEACCESSIONED FROM THE COLLECTIONS

This is a tremendously controversial issue in the museum field, so much so that it deserves considerable discussion here. When the AAM Code of Ethics for Museums was revised in 1991, it said such funds could only be used for the acquisition of new collections. This was one of two issues that were so contentious they led to the statement being recalled for further editing. (The other was the proviso that AAM would enforce its membership's compliance with the Code of Ethics, which went over like the proverbial lead balloon.) The version approved in 1993, after much wrangling, added the category of "direct care" to acquisitions as acceptable use of such funds, while leaving that term open to interpretation.

This question is not just an arcane, museum-profession issue—it is a hot button for the general public, as well. If you total all the controversies that land museums in the news, use of funds from the sale of deaccessioned material accounts for a large chunk of them. Even people not familiar with museum standards understand intuitively that museums hold collections in the public trust, and that collections are not financial assets to be used to balance the museum's books or make up for monetary shortfalls.

Further complicating matters is the fact that the federal government, specifically the Internal Revenue Service (IRS), together with the Financial Accounting Standards Board (FASB) and the Government Accounting Standards Board (GASB), takes an intense interest in this subject. FASB and GASB establish the standards that determine how auditors account for collections in financial reports, and the IRS establishes how museums report financial and nonfinancial assets on their tax forms. In the 1990s, FASB pushed hard to require museums to capitalize all collections on their balance sheets and report them as financial assets. AAM and others waded into this battle and managed to forestall the move to capitalize collections—this time.

It was a difficult battle because from the viewpoint of the IRS, museums are trying to have their cake and eat it, too. We take the moral high ground, claiming the collections are not financial assets and should not be treated as such in accounting. But then we want to be able to sell them and use the cash for various purposes. So FASB and GASB conceded this point only with the stipulations that museums have to make a choice:

Either restrict the use of funds from deaccessioning to acquisition of new collections (therefore keeping the value in the same class of artistic/scientific/historic assets), or use the funds for other things, as well, in which case you have to account for them as financial assets. If there is a perception that museums are generally not abiding by these rules (for example, using funds from the sale of deaccessioned material for conservation or replacing the boiler but not capitalizing the collections), the issue may well be revisited. Next time, the battle might be lost.

If the money resulting from the sale of deaccessioned collections is so contentious, then why do museums sell collections? It took a long time for people inside and outside the field to decide that it is acceptable to deaccession material from the collections *at all*. There has long been a strong feeling that accessioning something into the collections meant it should remain there forever, particularly in the case of donated material. No matter what the fine print on the donation form says, such acceptance seems to donors to be an implicit guarantee that their treasures will be cared for by the museum forever. It has become clear over the past few decades, however, that this principle is often at odds with the museum's obligation to make good use of its resources to benefit the public and take good care of its collections. Sometimes people make bad choices, and objects end up in a collection where they don't do anyone any earthly good, yet deplete time and resources. Museum missions change over time, and sometimes things that were a good fit a hundred years ago now fall outside the museum's scope. Sometimes a museum's reach has simply exceeded its grasp, and it has amassed collections it is unable to care for—deaccessioning into public or private hands may be more responsible than letting it deteriorate from inadequate stewardship.

But because collections are a special category of asset (cultural, scientific, artistic, rather than financial) there is a strong feeling that when something leaves the collection, any funds resulting from its sale should be used to replenish the value or utility of that category. If museums can use such funds to pay for other things, like fixing the front walk, funding education programs or underwriting the museum journal, it becomes tempting to raid the collections to supplement operating funds or the endowment. There is clear consensus in the field that this is a violation of a museum's fiduciary responsibility to raise those funds in other ways. It is fundamentally unacceptable to use collections as financial assets to sustain operational need. Selling objects from the collections in order to achieve maximum profit and to dedicate the sale proceeds to addressing long-term financial instability is an abrogation of the public trust.

But the specifics of how to apply this principle remain murky. If you accept that the museum may have good reason not to purchase new collections (no suitable material is available on the market, it is unethical to purchase such material, the museum is not adding to its collections), what can the funds be used for? Conserving existing collections may seem solid, but does this apply only to active conservation (treatment) or also to preventive conservation (which may rely heavily on archival storage materials, appropriate climate control and regular monitoring for pests)? Can it include salaries or fees for labor (such as the time of a conservator, curator or collections manager) related to preservation activities, even if such monies would be a normal part of the annual operating budget? If it is appropriate to use funds to improve conditions in storage, why not in exhibit areas? And since the museum building is an integral whole, does it not benefit the collections when the roof or electrical/mechanical/alarm/fire suppression systems are upgraded?

There are also many situations in which it is very, very tempting to chip away at the principle itself. What if the museum is going broke? The collections can't be taken care of if the whole institution goes downhill. For that matter (and this has happened), what if the museum is disposing of its collections because it is becoming a non–collections-based organization? These are not easy questions, and there are no easy answers, but exceptional cases cannot be used to establish the ethical principle that guides the mainstream of museum conduct.

MUSEUMS INSIDE NON-MUSEUM PARENT ORGANIZATIONS

Museum ethics guide the conduct of museums. What about their parent organizations? Is a university obligated to abide by museum ethics when setting policy or practice for one of its museums? Functionally, it is impossible for a small part of an organization (the museum) to dictate to a parent how it should behave. At best the museum can persuade the parent that it is ethically appropriate to let the museum abide by museum standards. Or it may point out that forcing the museum to violate the ethical guidelines people expect museums to abide by will generate bad press or endanger relations with alumni. The parent may value accreditation, and the museum might use accreditation enforcement of standards as a way to leverage compliance. In any case, it is useful to initiate these discussions prior to it actually becoming an issue. Usually parent organizations only engage in behavior their museums consider unethical if there is a significant incentive (monetary, political). It can be difficult to initiate open, unbiased discussions regarding standards of conduct for the organization once these factors are already in play.

II. Mission and Planning

STANDARDS REGARDING INSTITUTIONAL MISSION STATEMENTS

Characteristics of Excellence Related to Mission

▶ The museum asserts its public service role and places education at the center of that role.

▶ The museum is committed to public accountability and is transparent in its mission and its operations.

▶ The museum has a clear understanding of its mission and communicates why it exists and who benefits as a result of its efforts.

▶ All aspects of the museum's operations are integrated and focused on meeting its mission.

▶ The museum's governing authority and staff think and act strategically to acquire, develop and allocate resources to advance the mission of the museum.

PURPOSE AND IMPORTANCE

All museums are expected to have a formally stated and approved mission that states what the museum does, for whom and why. A museum's mission statement is the primary benchmark against which to evaluate the museum's performance. One of the two core questions underlying any assessment of compliance with national standards is: *How well does the museum achieve its stated mission and goals?* This emphasis acknowledges an effective and replicable practice: Museums that use clearly delineated mission statements to guide their activities and decisions are more likely to function effectively.

A clearly delineated mission statement guides museum activities and decisions by describing the purpose of a museum—its reason for existence. It defines the museum's unique identity and purpose, and provides a distinct focus for the institution. A mission statement articulates the museum's understanding of its role and responsibility to the public and its collections, and reflects the environment in which it exists. Activities of the museum should support, directly or indirectly, the mission.

Commentary

LENGTH

Sometimes museums trip over terminology when interpreting this standard. Some museums nowadays write short, punchy mission statements that fit on a business card or the footer of the museum's stationary. These can be inspiring, but sometimes a little vague on the specifics:

The increase and diffusion of knowledge among men.
—*Smithsonian Institution*, 1826

To invite learners of all ages to experience their changing world through science.
—*Science Museum of Minnesota*

Statements like these can be problematic in terms of describing the purpose of a museum, defining its unique identity and focus, etc., if only because of their brevity. Which isn't to say that there's not a place for statements like this (for example, on a business card or stationary). When museums write missions this brief, they may have another document (sometimes called a statement of purpose) that goes into more detail about what the museum does, for whom and why. In practice this is fine, as long as sufficient detail is captured somewhere, "sufficient" being enough to guide specific choices or assess whether the museum is meeting its mission. Other solutions might be to make the short statement a preamble to a more detailed mission statement, and then use it as an excerpt when appropriate; or have a longer mission statement and create a punchy, informal tag line that captures the spirit of the mission.

CONSISTENCY

One of the most common problems with mission statements is that if they change over time, different versions appear in different places, fossilized at the time of a given document's approval. The current statement may be in the institutional plan, but the collections policy, last revised a decade ago, contains an old version. Yet another appears in the fundraising plan (the development staff took the liberty of jazzing up the language a bit). This can be mere housekeeping, though still important, if the differences are trivial. But if the difference is substantive, reflecting a shift in what the museum has chosen to do, collect, or who it will serve, it is an extremely serious issue. The disparate versions may reflect a broader failure to review plans and policies comprehensively to make sure they are all working toward the same goal. And it may mean that parts of the staff that look to these documents for their marching orders are being sent in different directions.

REALISM

Another serious problem with mission statements arises when the goals they set for the museum exceed the museum's resources. It is wonderful to aspire to be one of the most important natural history museums in the country, but do you have the collections to support this? If not, do you have a big enough budget to build such a collection and support the necessary research? Assessment of museums against the standards is grounded in the mission-based goals they set for themselves—if the mission cannot plausibly be achieved, they have sunk themselves to begin with.

It may be more appropriate to write a mission statement that is within the museum's grasp, and capture the "blue sky" thinking in a vision statement that paints a picture of what the museum would like to be in the future. That way the museum is being judged in light of something it can do, while still presenting a compelling image of what the museum could become with sufficient support.

ALIGNMENT WITH THE PARENT INSTITUTION

Museums that exist within a larger parent organization—such as a college, university, foundation, religious institution or arm of government—face particular challenges. Since they probably don't have separate articles of incorporation, they did not have to declare a formal mission statement in order to receive nonprofit status. That leaves questions of who is going to write the mission statement, who is going to approve it and with what level of authority. This can create several different kinds of problems.

If the museum staff or advisory board is given considerable latitude, they may approve a good, realistic mission statement that they proceed to implement very well. This kind of benign neglect can sometimes seem like a blessing. But when money, space or staffing gets squeezed, the parent organization often looks at the museum and says, "Huh! Is that what you are doing? It is not crucially important to us, so you get cut first." On the other hand, the parent may exercise very tight control and create a mission statement for the museum that ignores great opportunities that the staff sees clearly and would like to pursue. For example, a college might direct its museum to put its attention solely on serving the student body. Seems reasonable, on the face of it. But the museum may be the college's best potential ambassador to the neighboring community, an important role if the town-gown relationship is strained to begin with.

These kinds of issues are best addressed by ensuring that some person or group with an appropriate level of authority in the parent organization (e.g., provost, dean, vice president) works closely with the museum staff and advisory board (if one exists) in reviewing and approving the museum's mission, and the plans built upon it. There should be a shared understanding of the museum's mission *before* making decisions about planning and resource allocation.

STANDARDS REGARDING INSTITUTIONAL PLANNING

Characteristics of Excellence Related to Planning

- ▶ All aspects of the museum's operations are integrated and focused on meeting its mission.
- ▶ The museum's governing authority and staff think and act strategically to acquire, develop and allocate resources to advance the mission of the museum.
- ▶ The museum engages in ongoing and reflective institutional planning that includes involvement of its audiences and community.
- ▶ The museum establishes measures of success and uses them to evaluate and adjust its activities.

PURPOSE AND IMPORTANCE

Strategic planning produces a mutually agreed-upon vision of where the museum is going and what it wants to achieve. It ensures this vision meets the needs of its audiences and community and that the museum identifies how it will obtain the resources to fulfill this vision. Planning allows the museum to make sound decisions in response to changes in its operating environment.

Museums use planning to set goals and establish strategies by which it will achieve them; to ensure that the museum acquires, develops and allocates its resources (human, financial, physical) in a way that advances its mission and sustains its financial viability; to gather appropriate information to guide its actions, including input from stakeholders and data from benchmarking; and to establish measures by which the museum will assess its achievements.

IMPLEMENTATION

Museums should engage in current, comprehensive, timely and formal planning for their future. Planning is current when it is up-to-date, and reflective of an ongoing process; comprehensive when it covers all relevant aspects of museum operations (e.g., not just a facility master plan); timely when it is geared to significant events in the museum's lifecycle (e.g., changes in size, scope, purpose, governance, etc.); formal when the process and outcome are documented in writing and approved by vote of the governing authority. The process should be inclusive of all stakeholders: staff, governing authority, audiences and community; ongoing; reflective; documented.

DOCUMENTATION

As evidence of its institutional planning, museums should have documentation of the planning process (e.g., committee lists, meeting minutes, planning schedules) and a current, comprehensive, timely and formal institutional plan that includes both strategic and operational elements. Each museum's written institutional plan should include a multiyear and an operational plan, a combination of the two or the functional equivalent.

Each museum's planning documents will look different. However, the plan(s) should: be captured in written documents and approved by the governing authority; be based on the mission; be tied to other relevant planning documents (e.g., financial plans, development plans, interpretive plans, collections plans); set priorities helping the museum make choices and allocate available resources; identify how the institution will secure the human and financial resources needed to implement the plan by bringing resources and goals into alignment; be living documents, continually used and updated by the staff and governing authority; establish measurable goals and methods by which the museum will evaluate success; and include action steps, establish timelines and assign responsibility for implementation.

PLANNING BY MUSEUMS WITHIN NON-MUSEUM PARENT ORGANIZATIONS
Museums operated by a parent organization for which museum management is not the primary purpose (e.g., a university, or government agency) are expected to have a museum/site-specific planning process and plan, both of which should be linked to the parent organization's planning. The parent organization's planning process and documents should also reflect support for the museum's mission and ensure that museum/site-specific goals can be achieved.

Commentary

WHY PLAN?

I am asked time and again, "Why does my museum need a plan? We are doing a great job without one." There are so many answers to this question it is hard to know where to begin. How do you know you are doing a great job if you have not decided as a group (board, staff, stakeholders) what that job is? If that decision is not written down and approved, how do you know you all really have the same understanding of what you intend to do and how to get there? What happens if the director (who is usually the driving force in the museum) leaves? How does the next director know what the plan is and how to keep it smoothly progressing in the right direction? Without a written plan, how do you convince (fill in the blank: the public, local government, philanthropists, charitable foundations, granting agencies) that what you intend to do is worth their support? This is just the short list—other reasons abound. The fact is, planning is necessary for your museum's continued survival—not only to increase the chances that you are going in the right direction but to leverage support. Very, very few foundations, corporations or granting agencies are going to give you funds nowadays unless you have a plan that meets the characteristics outlined in this standard.

PROCESS

Half of the value of a plan (maybe more than half) derives from the process of creating it. It is possible for one person to lock themselves in a room and concoct something that looks like an institutional plan, but it is likely to be a hollow document. Plans are more likely to be realistic, successful and well-implemented if the process of planning includes a diverse group of stakeholders including board members, staff, key supporters, members of the museum's self-identified community and neighbors. Why? The people the museum serves are the experts on whether the museum is serving them well and the best reality checkers about ideas on how to do this better. Plus, a group of people with diverse backgrounds, experience and training will consider a broader range of possibilities and do a better job analyzing the pros and cons of each. And staff, board, volunteers and community members are more likely to support the plan and do a good job implementing it if they have been involved in its development.

CONTENT

The standard regarding planning is one of the most specific standards developed through AAM. Why all the detail? It was principally written by the Accreditation Commission, which reviews about a hundred museums each year, sees the same museums once every ten years, and has tracked some museums for more than thirty years of their existence. This gives them extensive experience observing what causes museums to succeed (or fail), and how this ties to elements in their plans. Every specific element called for in the standard (priorities, timelines, resources, assignment of responsibility) is listed because its absence has been observed to be a stumbling block for many, many museums. Think of accreditation as a big, long-term scientific experiment. Accredited museums are the guinea pigs for all museums, testing what works and what doesn't work. And they are the highest-performing museums in the country, in the opinion of their peers. If planning is crucial to their success, why would it be any less important for the other 95 percent of museums?

If you are just beginning to write your plan, I suggest you use the standard to create an outline for its contents. If you have a plan, I suggest you review it against the standard and see if there are places it may need more detail.

III. Leadership and Organizational Structure

STANDARDS REGARDING GOVERNANCE
Characteristics of Excellence Related to Governance

▶ The governance, staff and volunteer structures and processes effectively advance the mission.

▶ The governing authority, staff and volunteers have a clear and shared understanding of their roles and responsibilities.

▶ The governing authority, staff and volunteers legally, ethically and effectively carry out their responsibilities.

▶ The composition and qualifications of the museum's leadership, staff and volunteers enable it to carry out the museum's mission and goals.

▶ There is a clear and formal division of responsibilities between the governing authority and any group that supports the museum, whether separately incorporated or operating within the museum or its parent organization.

PURPOSE AND IMPORTANCE

Good governance is the foundation that enables the museum to succeed. The effective operation of a museum is based on a well-functioning governing authority that has a strong working relationship with the museum director. Together, the governing authority and director set the direction of the museum, obtain and manage the resources needed for it to fulfill its mission and ensure that the museum is accountable to the public. These expectations apply to all museums regardless of governance type, structure or name.

IMPLEMENTATION

The governing authority fulfills the basic responsibilities of nonprofit governance by: determining the organization's mission and purposes; selecting the chief executive and supporting and assessing his or her performance; ensuring effective organizational planning and adequate resources; managing resources effectively (including exercising good stewardship of collections and historic structures, if applicable); ensuring that the organization's programs and services advance the mission; enhancing the organization's public standing; ensuring legal and ethical integrity and maintaining accountability; recruiting and orienting new members of the governing authority; and assessing performance of the governing authority. For museums that have remote governance, these responsibilities may be spread out along a designated chain of command. In such cases, responsibilities must be clearly assigned to particular positions. For museums with joint governance, these responsibilities may be partitioned between different entities. See below regarding national standards in these situations.

STANDARDS FOR MUSEUMS WITH JOINT GOVERNANCE

In museums with joint governance, in which the basic responsibilities of governance are shared between two or more groups (e.g., a city and a private, nonprofit organization, or a university and an advisory board), or when a separate entity provides resources vital to the museum's operation (e.g., land, collections, building, staff), the standards require that the museum clearly identify all the groups that are engaged in governance or provision of these vital resources, and the responsibilities of each group. These relationships should be detailed in formal, written documents (e.g., memoranda of agreement, memoranda of understanding, operating agreement).

DOCUMENTATION

As evidence that good governance practices are in place and to demonstrate that the museum is meeting the Characteristics of Excellence, museums should have the following documents: mission statement; institutional plan; articles of incorporation, charter, enabling legislation or other founding document; bylaws, constitution, will or other documentation under which the museum is governed. If the museum has a parent organization, it should have documentation regarding the importance of the museum to the parent, expressing its commitment to support the museum (e.g., resolution of permanence passed by parent, parent organization's bylaws or organizing documents, memorandum of understanding or management agreement between the parent and the museum). Museums should have documentation of operational relationships with other organizations integrally connected to the museum's governance or operations (e.g., written memorandum of understanding or other type of formal agreement) and evidence of delegation of authority for operation of the museum to the museum director or the equivalent position.

STANDARDS REGARDING THE COMPOSITION OF THE GOVERNING AUTHORITY

A governing authority is expected to: cycle in new people and new ideas; reflect the diversity of the communities it serves; provide opportunities for external input so that the governing authority is accountable to those communities; and ensure that members of the governing authority are evaluated on their performance and nonperforming members are cycled out. *There do not have to be term limits for the service of members of the governing authority,* though this is one method traditionally employed by museums to achieve these goals.

When it is not possible to control these factors within the governing authority itself (e.g., museums within parent organizations, those with remote governance or those that are government-governed), the museum needs to find other ways to accomplish the goals outlined above. This may include establishing supporting groups as needed to assist with governance (e.g., advisory boards, auxiliary groups, community boards).

Commentary

RESPONSIBILITIES OF THE NONPROFIT BOARD

This standard was written to focus board members' attention on the job that is uniquely theirs to do. The basic responsibilities of nonprofit governance listed under Implementation on page 40, are adapted from Richard Ingram's classic *Ten Basic Responsibilities of Nonprofit Governance,* and are widely accepted by all types of nonprofits, not just museums. But government and the public have ever higher expectations of the level of oversight provided by what are, essentially, untrained volunteers (they may be highly trained in their professions, but are rarely trained in nonprofit governance). Many of the scandals that have dogged nonprofits in general and museums in particular in the past decade stem from the failure of the governing authority to provide appropriate oversight. Examples include excessive compensation of the chief executive officer, provision of lavish perks or even outright fraud and abuse in reimbursement of expenses; failure to realize or act on the scope of the museum's financial difficulties or to detect misleading bookkeeping and reporting on the part of staff; and engaging in or allowing the museum to engage in actions that appear to involve conflicts of interest regarding staff, board, individual or corporate donors, lenders or for-profit entities. As board members rarely have formal training in nonprofit governance or museum standards, it usually falls to museum staff to educate them regarding these responsibilities, or at least to help establish the process by which each board trains incoming members.

REFLECTING THE DIVERSITY OF THE COMMUNITY

Diversity is one of many areas in which the national standards can provide general guidance, but each museum must decide for itself the appropriate way to apply the standards. Only the museum and its constituents can identify what aspects of diversity are relevant in their circumstances and what constitutes appropriate diversity for the museum's governance. We can say a bit about the opposite—common patterns of homogeneity, why they arise and persist, and the barriers they can pose to museum excellence.

A museum's founder or founders often influence the museum long after they have passed on. One way you can see this is to look at who serves on the board of trustees. Because most boards of separate 501(c)3 museums are self-perpetuating (though some are elected by the membership) they usually select members who look a lot like them. This is natural—people are usually more comfortable working with people who share their background and experiences. And they usually recruit new board members from their circle of existing acquaintances. But it is also a problem—see discussions of diversity on pages 22 and 60. And it can be self-perpetuating, as when the museum finally reaches out to groups that have not traditionally been invited to serve on the board, only to find that they have no interest in doing so. Some of the patterns of homogeneity that we often see in museums include: affluent, socially prominent older white men, and occasionally women, particularly in organizations that are prestigious and have considerable financial resources; enthusiasts/knowledgeable amateurs—for instance, railroad enthusiasts or antique car collectors; scholars/academics—such as historians or scientists; ethnically homogeneous members—particularly if the museum interprets a particular culture or ethnic group; genealogically linked members—notably found in museums run by groups such as the Daughters of the American Revolution, Colonial Dames, Sons of the Confederacy, etc. Any of these groups can bring strengths to governing their museums. But if they are the only people at the table, they are severely limited in their ability to see a bigger picture, access diverse resources, reach out to new constituencies and build the next generation of museum visitors and board members. This effect is made worse by the fact that any one of these variables (race, ethnicity, profession, interests) may bring with them other, unintended sources of homogeneity. For example, a board of academics and scholars may contribute formidable expertise about the museum's subject area but they may have limited financial resources or access to people with such resources.

JOINT GOVERNANCE

At least 4 percent of museums have some form of joint governance. This may be a college or municipal museum with a separate, private nonprofit friends group that raises essential funds, or even hires part of the staff and owns the collections. It may be a museum jointly run by a city, which owns the building and collections, and a private nonprofit group contracted to hire staff and operate the museum. Sometimes the entities are so intertwined it is impossible to point to just one of them and say, "That is the museum." The museum truly arises from their pooled efforts.

These arrangements are increasingly common as museums search for successful financial models. And they are frequently successful. However, they are vulnerable at the point of intersection. What if the arrangement between the two (or three or four) entities running the museum breaks down? What if the city says it wants to take its collections back and go make another museum elsewhere? What if the friends group decides it won't provide its annual contribution to the operating fund unless the museum exhibits the collections of the group's chairperson?

Many of these arrangements function in the first place because of the level of trust that exists between people in key positions of the cooperating entities. When those people eventually leave, everything can be thrown into the air. Personal relationships are transitory—legal agreements last (at least until they are dissolved by mutual agreement or broken in court). Some organizations hesitate to propose a formal agreement with the entity that partners with them to run the museum because "things work okay now, but we are afraid things will fall apart if we bring this up." This hardly inspires confidence about the stability of the arrangement. Often the best thing a museum can do to ensure that the relationship continues to function smoothly is to capture it in a written legal agreement, enabling both parties to work out, in advance of a dispute, how they mutually want things to function.

STANDARDS REGARDING DELEGATION OF AUTHORITY

All museums should have a director or the functional equivalent, part time or full time, paid or unpaid, to whom authority is delegated for day-to-day operations. Furthermore, the governing authority, staff and volunteers should have a clear and shared understanding of their roles and responsibilities.

PURPOSE AND IMPORTANCE

Having clear delegation of authority means that the governing authority understands the main areas of its responsibility. Those areas are to collectively determine mission, set policies for operations, ensure that charter and bylaw provisions are followed, plan for the institution, approve budgets, establish financial controls and ensure that adequate resources are available to advance the museum's mission.

Delegation of authority leads to effective leadership and organizational structure by creating clarity about the distinct roles of governance and management; this clarity allows each to focus on the work they need to do. There is communication and collaboration but no duplication of effort. Since the governing authority has appointed a director (or equivalent position) with the expertise to run the museum, it should allow the director to perform his or her responsibilities without interference.

An unencumbered line of authority allows the institution to achieve more. It promotes good use of resources, including time. The director has the authority to act independently and oversee the day-to-day operations while the governing authority uses its time to make decisions that steer the institution. Staff at all levels should be clear about the chain of command.

DOCUMENTATION

Documentation of the delegation of authority may be found in the bylaws of the institution, the formally approved job description of the director (or equivalent position) and, to apprise all staff, is often stated in the institution's staff handbook.

Commentary

DELEGATION OF AUTHORITY

You can infer, from the fact that there is a whole standard just about delegation of authority to the director that it is frequent source of tension in museums. People who serve on the governing authority, after all, do so because they are passionately interested in what the museum does. But the role assigned to the board—approving policies and budgets, planning, finding money—can seem pretty dry. If board members are lucky, they get to serve on a collections committee and shop with other people's money. But the really fun part—designing exhibits and programs, choosing the carpeting for the new wing—belongs to the staff. Is it any wonder that board members often start nudging their way into these staff functions? But doing so fatally undermines the authority of the director and the professionalism of the staff.

Delegation of authority can be especially hard to enforce in small museums run mostly or entirely by volunteers, particularly if some board members also serve as volunteers (curators, exhibit preparators, development officers or salespeople, etc.). These dual roles put them simultaneously above the director (as his or her boss and supervisor) and below (as a staff member). Many small museums operate this way, and it works well if individuals wearing two very different hats remember to switch their headgear as appropriate.

Delegation of authority can also be problematic in museums within larger parent organizations such as universities and city or state governments. Sometimes the temptation to reach down and tinker with the fun parts (exhibits, again, are ever popular, as are collections and collecting) is just overwhelming to administrators. This standard can help museum directors explain to the (fill in the blank: provost, city manager, mayor, governor) why their direct intervention in museum operations is inappropriate.

IV. Collections Stewardship

STANDARDS REGARDING COLLECTIONS STEWARDSHIP
Characteristics of Excellence Related to Collections Stewardship

▶ The museum owns, exhibits or uses collections that are appropriate to its mission.

▶ The museum legally, ethically and effectively manages, documents, cares for and uses the collections.

▶ The museum conducts collections-related research according to appropriate scholarly standards.

▶ The museum strategically plans for the use and development of its collections.

▶ The museum, guided by its mission, provides public access to its collections while ensuring their preservation.

▶ The museum allocates its space and uses its facilities to meet the needs of the collections, audience and staff.

▶ The museum has appropriate measures in place to ensure the safety and security of people, its collections and/or objects, and the facilities it owns or uses.

▶ The museum takes appropriate measures to protect itself against potential risk and loss.

PURPOSE AND IMPORTANCE

Stewardship is the careful, sound and responsible management of that which is entrusted to a museum's care. Possession of collections incurs legal, social and ethical obligations to provide proper physical storage, management and care for the collections and associated documentation, as well as proper intellectual control. Collections are held in trust for the public and made accessible for the public's benefit. Effective collections stewardship ensures that the objects the museum owns, borrows, holds in its custody and/or uses are available and accessible to present and future generations. A museum's collections are an important means of advancing its mission and serving the public.

IMPLEMENTATION

Museums are expected to: plan strategically and act ethically with respect to collections stewardship matters; legally, ethically and responsibly acquire, manage and dispose of collection items as well as know what collections are in its ownership/custody, where they came from, why it has them and their current condition and location; and provide regular and reasonable access to, and use of, the collections/objects in its custody.

Achieving this standard requires thorough understanding of collections stewardship issues to ensure thoughtful and responsible planning and decision making. With this in mind, national standards emphasize systematic development and regular review of policies, procedures, practices and plans for the goals, activities and needs of the collections.

HOW DOES A MUSEUM ASSESS WHETHER ITS COLLECTIONS AND/OR OBJECTS ARE APPROPRIATE FOR ITS MISSION?

This is determined by comparing the institution's mission—how it formally defines its unique identity and purpose, and its understanding of its role and responsibility to the public—to two things: (1) the collections used by the institution; and (2) its policies, procedures and practices regarding the development and use of collections (see also the Standards Regarding Institutional Mission Statements).

A review of a museum's collections stewardship practices examines: whether the mission statement or collections documents (e.g., collections management policy, collections plan, etc.) are clear enough to guide collections stewardship decisions; whether the collections owned by the museum, and objects loaned and exhibited at the museum, fall within the scope of the stated mission and collections documents; and whether the mission and other collections stewardship-related documents are in alignment and guide the museum's practices.

ASSESSING COLLECTIONS STEWARDSHIP

There are different ways to manage, house, secure, document and conserve collections, depending on their media and use, and the museum's own discipline, size, physical facilities, geographic location and financial and human resources. Therefore, one must consider many facets of an institution's operations that, taken together, demonstrate the effectiveness of its collections stewardship policies, procedures and practices, and assess them in light of varying factors. For instance, museums may have diverse types of collections categorized by different levels of purpose and use—permanent, educational, archival, research and study, to name a few—that may have different management and care needs. These distinctions should be articulated in collections stewardship-related policies and procedures. In addition, different museum disciplines may have different collections stewardship practices, issues and needs related to their specific field. Museums are expected to follow the standards and best practices appropriate to their respective discipline and/or museum type as applicable.

The standards require that:

▶ A current, approved, comprehensive collections management policy is in effect and actively used to guide the museum's stewardship of its collections.

▶ The human resources are sufficient, and the staff have the appropriate education, training and experience to fulfill the museum's stewardship responsibilities and the needs of the collections.

▶ Staff are delegated responsibility to carry out the collections management policy.

▶ A system of documentation, records management and inventory is in effect to describe each object and its acquisition (permanent or temporary), current condition and location and movement into, out of and within the museum.

▶ The museum regularly monitors environmental conditions and takes proactive measures to mitigate the effects of ultraviolet light, fluctuations in temperature and humidity, air pollution, damage, pests and natural disasters on collections.

- An appropriate method for identifying needs and determining priorities for conservation/care is in place.

- Safety and security procedures and plans for collections in the museum's custody are documented, practiced and addressed in the museum's emergency/disaster preparedness plan.

- Regular assessment of, and planning for, collection needs (development, conservation, risk management, etc.) takes place and sufficient financial and human resources are allocated for collections stewardship.

- Collections care policies and procedures for collections on exhibition, in storage, on loan and during travel are appropriate, adequate and documented.

- The scope of a museum's collections stewardship extends to both the physical and intellectual control of its property.

- Ethical considerations of collections stewardship are incorporated into the appropriate museum policies and procedures.

- Considerations regarding future collecting activities are incorporated into institutional plans and other appropriate policy documents.

Commentary

COLLECTIONS STEWARDSHIP:
THE BIG PICTURE, AND THEN THE DETAILS . . .

No other area of museum standards is backed up by more technical literature, interpreting every nuance to the nth degree. Perversely enough, this can make it more difficult, not less, to adapt the standards to the museum's mission, goals and circumstances, as specified by the "Two Core Questions." Reams of research have been published on the effects of temperature and humidity on a variety of materials. The pros and cons of wet pipe versus dry pipe (not to mention pre-action) fire suppression systems have been endlessly debated. None of this helps a small, local historical society clearly answer the question: "What climate control (if any) or fire suppression (ditto) should we install in our historic, one-room schoolhouse?" Because it is all too easy to become bogged down in a morass of detail, for this area of the standards it is particularly useful to start with the big picture, as baldly stated in the Characteristics of Excellence in Translation:

Know what stuff you have.

Know what stuff you need.

Know where it is.

Take good care of it.

Make sure someone gets some good out of it . . .

Especially people you care about . . .

And your neighbors.

This big-picture view keeps you focused on outcomes rather than methods. The museum staff can then thoughtfully choose benchmarks for the desired results, and work backwards from that to the appropriate details of implementation, factoring in the museum's resources, both human and financial.

For example, "Know what stuff you have" refers to records-keeping and inventory, of course. The museum needs records (paper and/or electronic) of what it owns, its origin, significance, history of use, location and condition. Before you leap into an online debate with your colleagues on Museum-L about the relative merits of cataloguing software, stop and assess the scope of your collection and what you are doing with it. Is your museum a small, all-volunteer historic house with 200 objects that does not loan or borrow material? Maybe it is enough for you to make a duplicate copy of your physical card catalogue (on archival card stock, of course) to keep off-site. On the other hand, if you have a paleontology collection with a few hundred thousand specimens, and its primary users are international researchers, you may need a first-class relational database capable of publishing catalogue data to the Web in a searchable format, compatible with any relevant data standards. If you curate an art museum, you may need digital visual documentation of every work of art, of a quality suitable both for scholarly use and insurance purposes. As with all areas of collections care, the appropriate solution can only be assessed relative to the collections, their needs, their users and the museum's mission and resources.

CLIMATE CONTROL

Climate control is a particularly contentious issue, both because the associated mechanical systems can soak up a seemingly endless supply of funds to design, build, adjust and maintain, and because there is no absolute standard for "correct" climate control. For one thing, museums usually store and display more than one kind of collection, and different materials (pottery, fabric, painted wooden panels, furniture, taxidermy specimens, minerals, fluid specimens) have different optimal conditions for temperature and relative humidity. It is rarely practical for museums to have a storage room with separately adjustable climate controls for each and every material type. Even if you can afford a climate-control system that can maintain precisely whatever climate you choose, the settings are a compromise between the needs of these different collections.

For another thing, climate control is a classic example of "the perfect is the enemy of the good." Climate-control systems are expensive, and complex systems are notoriously finicky and difficult to maintain. Many museums might be better off installing a serviceable, resilient system that does a pretty good job of maintaining a set point with acceptable fluctuations, and putting the money they did not spend on a "state of the art" system into materials and labor to create microclimates (cases, plastic bags, desiccants) or provide quality pest management or security. "Taking good care of it" is the cumulative effect of a balanced approach to all these actions.

For museums that exist in, or primarily are, historic houses or sites, climate-control systems can actually be destructive, not only to the historic integrity but also to the actual fabric of the house. While the historic house community is currently working to formulate standards on this issue, there is already consensus that minimal climate control is often the appropriate approach for certain historic structures. Opening and closing the windows at the right times of the year, thus using the "passive control" systems a house was designed to exploit, may be both historically appropriate and the most effective way to conserve some buildings. What about the furnishings, costumes, archives and other materials that may be housed in such a structure? It might be more responsible for the organization to make strategic choices about displaying replicas or storing and displaying certain works in a separate, climate-controlled modern building.

Even in buildings that are merely functional rather than intrinsically historic in value, theoretical "best temperature and humidity" may be neither practical nor desirable. In climates with naturally very low humidity, trying to maintain 55 percent RH in the museum could be disastrous to the museum's energy bill and to the building. A brick building can literally pull itself to pieces in such conditions, as the interior moisture migrates through the walls to the outer, drier environment.

COLLECTIONS PLANNING

The good news about collections stewardship is that most of the problems museums encounter (overcrowded storage, need for climate control, staff for records-keeping, care, cleaning and pest control, etc.) can be solved simply with money. Not that money is necessarily easy to get, but at least the right solution is pretty straightforward once you consult the literature, confer with colleagues and make some rational choices. This is unlike some areas of performance such as governance, for which the problems tend to be interpersonal and political—and much harder to solve! (For example, a founding board that is unwilling to step aside for the new generation or adapt to the museum's changing needs—that one is not going to get fixed by something as simple as money.)

There is one big, thorny problem, however, in collections stewardship that money, per se, can't solve: "Know what stuff you need." Many museums (perhaps the majority) spend part of their precious resources taking care of materials that do not advance their mission, serve their audiences or support the exhibits, educational or research plans. This comes about for entirely understandable reasons. Many museums have legacy collections dating back to the founder, whose original vision for the museum may be far different from the role it plays now. Many museums built their collections over decades by accepting what was offered, often with no guiding template other than: "It fits our (very broad) mission, and it is neat stuff." With infinite resources, such materials would not be a problem. It might even (to paraphrase a frequent justification for keeping it) "be of some use someday." But no museum (not even the Smithsonian or the Getty) has infinite resources—there is always a limit to the time, space and money a museum has to care for collections and make them accessible, and all collections it cares for compete for these resources.

Collections planning is the process of making conscious, proactive choices about what belongs in the collections in light of the museum's mission, purposes and audiences. It actively shapes the collections to support the stories the museum intends to tell or the questions its users ask. While national standards do not yet call for all museums to have a collections plan, there is a growing consensus that it is a core document that helps the museum make wise choices and assures key supporters that the museum is making thoughtful use of the resources they contribute. Within the next decade, a collections plan will probably be as de rigueur as a collections management policy.

BEST PRACTICES REGARDING LOANING COLLECTIONS TO NON-MUSEUM ENTITIES

Museums hold collections in trust for the public. As stewards, museums fulfill their fiduciary and ethical responsibilities by preserving, caring for and providing access to collection objects for the benefit of the public. AAM recognizes that some museums loan objects from their collection to non-museum entities and encourages museums that do so to consider best practices for collections care and accessibility, and public accountability.

In some instances, loaning objects from the collection to non-museum entities may jeopardize the level of care provided for the items. This may constitute a breach of a museum's public trust responsibility and be perceived as an inappropriate or unethical use of objects held and maintained for the benefit of the public. Further, loaning objects from the collection to non-museum entities may result in inappropriate or inadequate practices in collections documentation and limit public access to the items.

If a museum engages in the practice of loaning objects from the collection to organizations other than museums, such a practice should be considered for its appropriateness to the museum's mission; be thoughtfully managed with the utmost care and in compliance with the most prudent practices in collections stewardship, ensuring that loaned objects receive the level of care, documentation and control at least equal to that given to the objects that remain on the museum premises; and be governed by clearly defined and approved institutional policies and procedures, including a collections management policy and code of ethics.

Commentary

Museums are often pressured by key supporters to lend to non-museum entities. This could be another nonprofit (schools, universities, hospitals, foundations), a for-profit business or a government entity. For example, a local bank that is a major donor to the museum may request a loan of art to hang in its corporate headquarters. A municipal museum may be expected to loan fine or decorative art to the mayor's office or official residence. While some people wish museums could agree that this is wrong, which would enable staff to cite national standards when they deny such requests, it isn't that simple. In some cases these loans may advance the museum's mission by reaching key audiences and expanding their opportunities to exhibit collections. In some cases it is political reality that such loans will take place. Responsible practices call for the museum to distinguish between acceptable uses (for example, displays in a climate-controlled, secure public space of a school, business or government building) that serve the public, and uses that may benefit individuals or private companies at the expense of the public good.

STANDARDS AND BEST PRACTICES REGARDING THE UNLAWFUL APPROPRIATION OF OBJECTS DURING THE NAZI ERA

This area of collections stewardship is of such sensitivity and high importance that it has separate standards and best-practice statements regarding a museum's obligations. These statements have been promulgated by the field to provide guidance to museums in fulfilling their public trust responsibilities.

Standards Regarding the Unlawful Appropriation of Objects During the Nazi Era

The reader is directed to the AAM website (www.aam-us.org) for a text of the standards that includes an introduction and history of how they were formulated, as well as AAM's commitment to supporting implementation.

General Principles

The American Association of Museums (AAM), the U.S. National Committee of the International Council of Museums (ICOM-US), and the American museum community are committed to continually identifying and achieving the highest standard of legal and ethical collections stewardship practices. The AAM Code of Ethics for Museums states that the "stewardship of collections entails the highest public trust and carries with it the presumption of rightful ownership, permanence, care, documentation, accessibility, and responsible disposal."

When faced with the possibility that an object in a museum's custody might have been unlawfully appropriated as part of the abhorrent practices of the Nazi regime, the museum's responsibility to practice ethical stewardship is paramount. Museums should develop and implement policies and practices that address this issue in accordance with these guidelines.

These guidelines are intended to assist museums in addressing issues relating to objects that may have been unlawfully appropriated during the Nazi era (1933–1945) as a result of actions in furtherance of the Holocaust or that were taken by the Nazis or their collaborators. For the purposes of these guidelines, objects that were acquired through theft, confiscation, coercive transfer or other methods of wrongful expropriation may be considered to have been unlawfully appropriated, depending on the specific circumstances.

In order to aid in the identification and discovery of unlawfully appropriated objects that may be in the custody of museums, the Presidential Advisory Commission on Holocaust Assets in the United States (PCHA), Association of Art Museum Directors (AAMD), and AAM have agreed that museums should strive to: (1) identify all objects in their collections that were created before 1946 and acquired by the museum after 1932, that underwent a change of ownership between 1932 and 1946, and that were or might reasonably be thought to have been in continental Europe between those dates (hereafter, "covered objects"); (2) make currently available object and provenance (history of ownership) information on those objects accessible; and (3) give priority to continuing provenance research as resources allow. AAM, AAMD and PCHA also agreed that the initial focus of research should be European paintings and Judaica.

Because of the Internet's global accessibility, museums are encouraged to expand online access to collection information that could aid in the discovery of objects unlawfully appropriated during the Nazi era without subsequent restitution.

AAM and ICOM-US acknowledge that during World War II and the years following the end of the war, much of the information needed to establish provenance and prove ownership was dispersed or lost. In determining whether an object may have been unlawfully appropriated without restitution, reasonable consideration should be given to gaps or ambiguities in provenance in light of the passage of time and the circumstances of the Holocaust era. AAM and ICOM-US support efforts to make archives and other resources more accessible and to establish databases that help track and organize information.

AAM urges museums to handle questions of provenance on a case-by-case basis in light of the complexity of this problem. Museums should work to produce information that will help to clarify the status of objects with an uncertain Nazi-era provenance. Where competing interests may arise, museums should strive to foster a climate of cooperation, reconciliation and commonality of purpose.

AAM affirms that museums act in the public interest when acquiring, exhibiting and studying objects. These guidelines are intended to facilitate the desire and ability of museums to act ethically and lawfully as stewards of the objects in their care, and should not be interpreted to place an undue burden on the ability of museums to achieve their missions.

Standards

1. Acquisitions

It is the position of AAM that museums should take all reasonable steps to resolve the Nazi-era provenance status of objects before acquiring them for their collections—whether by purchase, gift, bequest or exchange.

   a. Standard research on objects being considered for acquisition should include a request that the sellers, donors or estate executors offering an object provide as much provenance information as they have available, with particular regard to the Nazi era.
   b. Where the Nazi-era provenance is incomplete or uncertain for a proposed acquisition,

the museum should consider what additional research would be prudent or necessary to resolve the Nazi-era provenance status of the object before acquiring it. Such research may involve consulting appropriate sources of information, including available records and outside databases that track information concerning unlawfully appropriated objects.

c. In the absence of evidence of unlawful appropriation without subsequent restitution, the museum may proceed with the acquisition. Currently available object and provenance information about any covered object should be made public as soon as practicable after the acquisition.

d. If credible evidence of unlawful appropriation without subsequent restitution is discovered, the museum should notify the donor, seller or estate executor of the nature of the evidence and should not proceed with acquisition of the object until taking further action to resolve these issues. Depending on the circumstances of the particular case, prudent or necessary actions may include consulting with qualified legal counsel and notifying other interested parties of the museum's findings.

e. AAM acknowledges that under certain circumstances acquisition of objects with uncertain provenance may reveal further information about the object and may facilitate the possible resolution of its status. In such circumstances, the museum may choose to proceed with the acquisition after determining that it would be lawful, appropriate and prudent and provided that currently available object and provenance information is made public as soon as practicable after the acquisition.

f. Museums should document their research into the Nazi-era provenance of acquisitions.

g. Consistent with current practice in the museum field, museums should publish, display or otherwise make accessible recent gifts, bequests and purchases, thereby making all acquisitions available for further research, examination and public review and accountability.

2. Loans

It is the position of AAM that in their role as temporary custodians of objects on loan, museums should be aware of their ethical responsibility to consider the status of material they borrow as well as the possibility of claims being brought against a loaned object in their custody.

a. Standard research on objects being considered for incoming loan should include a request that lenders provide as much provenance information as they have available, with particular regard to the Nazi era.

b. Where the Nazi-era provenance is incomplete or uncertain for a proposed loan, the museum should consider what additional research would be prudent or necessary to resolve the Nazi-era provenance status of the object before borrowing it.

c. In the absence of evidence of unlawful appropriation without subsequent restitution, the museum may proceed with the loan.

STANDARDS AND BEST PRACTICES

d. If credible evidence of unlawful appropriation without subsequent restitution is discovered, the museum should notify the lender of the nature of the evidence and should not proceed with the loan until taking further action to clarify these issues. Depending on the circumstances of the particular case, prudent or necessary actions may include consulting with qualified legal counsel and notifying other interested parties of the museum's findings.

e. AAM acknowledges that in certain circumstances public exhibition of objects with uncertain provenance may reveal further information about the object and may facilitate the resolution of its status. In such circumstances, the museum may choose to proceed with the loan after determining that it would be lawful and prudent and provided that the available provenance about the object is made public.

f. Museums should document their research into the Nazi-era provenance of loans.

3. Existing Collections

It is the position of AAM that museums should make serious efforts to allocate time and funding to conduct research on covered objects in their collections whose provenance is incomplete or uncertain. Recognizing that resources available for the often lengthy and arduous process of provenance research are limited, museums should establish priorities, taking into consideration available resources and the nature of their collections.

Research

a. Museums should identify covered objects in their collections and make public currently available object and provenance information.

b. Museums should review the covered objects in their collections to identify those whose characteristics or provenance suggest that research be conducted to determine whether they may have been unlawfully appropriated during the Nazi era without subsequent restitution.

c. In undertaking provenance research, museums should search their own records thoroughly and, when necessary, contact established archives, databases, art dealers, auction houses, donors, scholars and researchers who may be able to provide Nazi-era provenance information.

d. Museums should incorporate Nazi-era provenance research into their standard research on collections.

e. When seeking funds for applicable exhibition or public programs research, museums are encouraged to incorporate Nazi-era provenance research into their proposals. Depending on their particular circumstances, museums are also encouraged to pursue special funding to undertake Nazi-era provenance research.

f. Museums should document their research into the Nazi-era provenance of objects in their collections.

NATIONAL STANDARDS AND BEST PRACTICES FOR U.S. MUSEUMS   55

Discovery of Evidence of Unlawfully Appropriated Objects

g. If credible evidence of unlawful appropriation without subsequent restitution is discovered through research, the museum should take prudent and necessary steps to resolve the status of the object, in consultation with qualified legal counsel. Such steps should include making such information public and, if possible, notifying potential claimants.

h. In the event that conclusive evidence of unlawful appropriation without subsequent restitution is found but no valid claim of ownership is made, the museum should take prudent and necessary steps to address the situation, in consultation with qualified legal counsel. These steps may include retaining the object in the collection or otherwise disposing of it.

i. AAM acknowledges that retaining an unclaimed object that may have been unlawfully appropriated without subsequent restitution allows a museum to continue to care for, research and exhibit the object for the benefit of the widest possible audience and provides the opportunity to inform the public about the object's history. If the museum retains such an object in its collection, it should acknowledge the object's history on labels and publications.

4. Claims of Ownership

It is the position of AAM that museums should address claims of ownership asserted in connection with objects in their custody openly, seriously, responsively and with respect for the dignity of all parties involved. Each claim should be considered on its own merits.

a. Museums should review promptly and thoroughly a claim that an object in its collection was unlawfully appropriated during the Nazi era without subsequent restitution.

b. In addition to conducting their own research, museums should request evidence of ownership from the claimant in order to assist in determining the provenance of the object.

c. If a museum determines that an object in its collection was unlawfully appropriated during the Nazi era without subsequent restitution, the museum should seek to resolve the matter with the claimant in an equitable, appropriate and mutually agreeable manner.

d. If a museum receives a claim that a borrowed object in its custody was unlawfully appropriated without subsequent restitution, it should promptly notify the lender and should comply with its legal obligations as temporary custodian of the object in consultation with qualified legal counsel.

e. When appropriate and reasonably practical, museums should seek methods other than litigation (such as mediation) to resolve claims that an object was unlawfully appropriated during the Nazi era without subsequent restitution.

f. AAM acknowledges that in order to achieve an equitable and appropriate resolution of claims, museums may elect to waive certain available defenses.

5. Fiduciary Obligations

Museums affirm that they hold their collections in the public trust when undertaking the activities listed above. Their stewardship duties and their responsibilities to the public they serve require that any decision to acquire, borrow, or dispose of objects be taken only after the completion of appropriate steps and careful consideration.

a. Toward this end, museums should develop policies and practices to address the issues discussed in these guidelines.

b. Museums should be prepared to respond appropriately and promptly to public and media inquiries.

Best Practices Regarding the Unlawful Appropriation of Objects During the Nazi Era

Public awareness of the extent to which cultural property was unlawfully appropriated during the Nazi era is greater than ever. Though much of the property was recovered and returned, or its owners compensated, there is still material unaccounted for. Therefore, the museum community strives to identify this material in order that restitution may be made.

Because they hold their collections in trust for the public, it is important for museums to identify this material. Stewardship of collections "carries with it the presumption of rightful ownership, permanence, care, documentation, accessibility and responsible disposal," as articulated in the AAM Code of Ethics for Museums. AAM views the issue of unlawful appropriation of objects during the Nazi era as one of high significance for all museums.

Museums are directed to the Standards Concerning the Unlawful Appropriation of Objects During the Nazi Era, developed in 1999 by a joint working group appointed by the AAM Board of Directors and ICOM-US Board. Museums are also directed to AAM Recommended Procedures for Providing Information to the Public about Objects Transferred in Europe During the Nazi Era, formulated pursuant to an agreement reached in October 2000 between AAM, the Association of Art Museum Directors (AAMD), and the Presidential Advisory Commission on Holocaust Assets in the United States (PCHA).

Museums are encouraged to register and participate in the Nazi-Era Provenance Internet Portal (NEPIP). This website (www.nepip.org) provides a searchable registry of objects in U.S. museum collections that were created before 1946 and changed hands in Continental Europe during the Nazi era (1933–1945). By participating in the Portal, museums that have such objects in their collections fulfill their responsibility under the Guidelines and Recommended Procedures adopted by the museum field to make Nazi-era provenance information accessible.

Commentary

Wrestling with the ethical dimensions of material that may have been unlawfully appropriated during the Nazi era has served as a prelude for the museum field to the more general issue of claims regarding cultural property. The standards regarding Nazi-era assets set an example for how such ethical decisions can be approached.

At the very least a museum should be aware of the origin of the material it might acquire, research these issues and make a thoughtful decision in alignment with its mission, policies and values that it is able and willing to explain to the public. Remember the Standards in Translation—being good means more than just following the law. Museums are obliged to consider ethical implications of their actions and weigh whether the outcomes they pursue are defensible in the court of public opinion, as well as the court of law.

The manner in which a museum treats claimants sets the tone for how this relationship will play out—and may determine whether the issue is resolved through mediation or goes to court. Handling claims promptly and respectfully can lead to relatively amicable and mutually productive discussions. Appropriate steps for a museum include promptly reviewing the claim, conducting its own research and asking for the claimant's research. If the object is in the museum's collection and there is credible evidence of unlawful appropriation without restitution, the museum should seek to resolve the matter with the claimant.

In many cases, a museum may have options to perfect its legal title to an object by invoking a narrow, technical defense in court (such as expiration of a statute of limitations). Museums should not resort to such defenses until they have first achieved an ethical determination based on an examination of all the available research. The availability of technical legal defenses is not an invitation to invoke the law to thwart an ethical outcome.

V. Education and Interpretation

STANDARDS REGARDING EDUCATION AND INTERPRETATION
Characteristics of Excellence Related to Education and Interpretation

- ▶ The museum clearly states its overall educational goals, philosophy and messages, and demonstrates that its activities are in alignment with them.
- ▶ The museum understands the characteristics and needs of its existing and potential audiences and uses this understanding to inform its interpretation.
- ▶ The museum's interpretive content is based on appropriate research.
- ▶ Museums conducting primary research do so according to scholarly standards.
- ▶ The museum uses techniques, technologies and methods appropriate to its educational goals, content, audiences and resources.
- ▶ The museum presents accurate and appropriate content for each of its audiences.
- ▶ The museum demonstrates consistent high quality in its interpretive activities.
- ▶ The museum assesses the effectiveness of its interpretive activities and uses those results to plan and improve its activities.

Commentary

Considering that education and interpretation are the core of all museums' activities, it may seem a bit surprising that there is little in the way of detailed standards, beyond the above Characteristics, elaborating on what museums must do to fulfill their basic obligations in this area of operation. (See Standards Regarding Exhibiting Borrowed Objects, which does provide additional commentary on a narrow but important issue, p. 61.) I offer the following observations on why this may be so.

First, museums are generally pretty good at education and interpretation. Remember I said at the beginning of this book that standards evolve to address things that are actually problems. Perhaps, as a field, we have not developed standards in this area because we do not feel there is any difficulty to be addressed. Second, there is no consensus on objective criteria for what constitutes "good education" or "good interpretation." At the narrow, technical level there are guidelines on writing and designing labels or building accessible exhibits, but is there really only one good way to write an exhibit label? To teach a program? To deliver content via the Web? Finally, this standard is another area where "good" can only be assessed in the context of the museum's mission, audiences and resources. You can't measure it by volume—a little museum mounting one changing exhibit a year and producing four public programs may be doing a better job, and making better use of its resources, than a similar museum that strains its finances and staff to produce three changing exhibits and twelve programs.

I can offer a few observations, however, about aspects of education and interpretation that often present challenges to many museums.

DIVERSITY OF AUDIENCE

Some museums were founded to serve the interests of a rather specific, sometimes narrowly defined, community. The unifying characteristic might be culture (Swedish Americans), interests (aviation enthusiasts) or genealogy (Daughters of the American Revolution). From one perspective, this is a museum's choice—each museum identifies its own mission and audience. Many feel, however, that if this audience is too narrowly defined the museum is, in effect, excluding people potentially interested in their topic, and therefore not serving the interests of the public in a broad sense. And it is the public, as a whole, that supports the museum through its tax-exempt status. On a practical level, few museums can afford to serve a narrowly defined audience, particularly as the demographic of any community tends to change over time, through aging, migration and shifts in interest. The smaller the group served by the museum, the more likely it is to find itself marginalized and without viable support.

Thus the Characteristics specify that a museum "understand the characteristics and needs of . . . its potential audiences" and that "the museum strives to be inclusive and offers opportunities for diverse participation." This paints a picture of an institution that tries to engage a broad variety of users, which will influence the stories and messages the museum chooses to tell and how it delivers them. For example, a historic house museum that focuses solely on the business and political accomplishments of its well-off, Caucasian, male owner may be missing aspects of interpretation that would engage the attention of other audiences—the stories of the women who managed the household, or the servants or slaves who made this lifestyle possible. Railroad enthusiasts may focus primarily on technological achievements, when there are broader stories to be told about economics, migration and social and geographic mobility, to name a few.

EVALUATION

In the absence of well-defined standards for education or interpretation, the most meaningful assessment is to measure whether it is working! The Accreditation Commission, in wrestling with standards for interpretation, has returned again and again to the thought that it would be sufficient if museums (a) defined what they wanted to achieve through their interpretive activities (interpretive planning); (b) measured whether they achieved their goals; and, of course, (c) took corrective action if necessary. Unfortunately, evaluation challenges many museums, even large ones with significant resources. There is an abundance of literature, many consultants and a plethora of evaluation schema to assist museums in this area. The best advice I have for museums wanting to demonstrate excellence in education and interpretation is to invest in a systematic, formal, ongoing program of evaluation for exhibits, programs and other interpretive activities, and to use the results of this evaluation to guide improvements in this area of operations.

STANDARDS REGARDING EXHIBITING BORROWED OBJECTS

The reader is directed to the AAM website (www.aam-us.org) for a copy of the standard that includes a preamble and history of the development of this standard.

Before considering exhibiting borrowed objects, a museum should have in place a written policy, approved by its governing authority and publicly accessible on request, that addresses the following issues:

1. Borrowing Objects

The policy will contain provisions:

a. Ensuring that the museum determines that there is a clear connection between the exhibition of the object(s) and the museum's mission, and that the inclusion of the object(s) is consistent with the intellectual integrity of the exhibition.

b. Requiring the museum to examine the lender's relationship to the institution to determine if there are potential conflicts of interest or an appearance of a conflict, such as in cases where the lender has a formal or informal connection to museum decision making (for example, as a board member, staff member or donor).

c. Including guidelines and procedures to address such conflicts or the appearance of conflicts or influence. Such guidelines and procedures may require withdrawal from the decision-making process of those with a real or perceived conflict, extra vigilance by decision makers, disclosure of the conflict or declining the loan.

d. Prohibiting the museum from accepting any commission or fee from the sale of objects borrowed for exhibition. This prohibition does not apply to displays of objects explicitly organized for the sale of those objects, for example craft shows.

2. Lender Involvement

The policy should assure that the museum will maintain intellectual integrity and institutional control over the exhibition. In following its policy, the museum:

a. should retain full decision-making authority over the content and presentation of the exhibition;

b. may, while retaining the full decision-making authority, consult with a potential lender on objects to be selected from the lender's collection and the significance to be given to those objects in the exhibition;

c. should make public the source of funding when the lender is also a funder of the exhibition. If a museum receives a request for anonymity, the museum should avoid such anonymity where it would conceal a conflict of interest (real or perceived) or raise other ethical issues.

Commentary

Why is the subject of borrowing objects—out of all the areas of performance related to education and interpretation—the one singled out for an explicit standard? Because it is one that often lands museums in the news, and not in a good way. It manages to hit many of the hot buttons that attract the attention of the press, the public, regulators and funders: conflict of interest, private profit subsidized by public support, integrity and trustworthiness of content.

And it illustrates the fact that we write standards to deal with things that actually happen. Notably, one famous incident that occurred just prior to the writing of this standard was the "Sensations" exhibition at the Brooklyn Museum. In that case, Charles Saatchi, noted collector of edgy, young British artists, lent his collection to the museum for a major exhibition. There were two areas of controversy surrounding this exhibit—the biggest public outcry was actually about content. (The Catholic community particularly objected to the work "Holy Virgin Mary" by Chris Ofili, which incorporated elephant dung and cutouts of female genitalia from pornographic magazines.) However, it also raised issues about process. The museum initially did not divulge that Saatchi, in addition to lending the works, both exerted considerable control over the curatorial content and provided significant financial support. Taken together with the fact that, to a degree unusual among collectors, Saatchi has a reputation for "flipping" collections (selling large portions after they have appreciated in value), it looked to the press, public and the mayor of the New York City as if Saatchi were perhaps using the museum, which receives considerable city funding, for his private benefit.

This case also illustrates one of the reasons compelling museums to develop their own voluntary standards. It is tempests like these that create the greatest risk of government (federal, state or local) stepping in to impose outside control over abuses of the public trust. And while the "Sensations" case may seem like a very specific (and extreme) example, the general issue arises quite often. Some other examples: A staff member, volunteer or board member is willing to lend a collection for an exhibit. Is there a perception that this inflates the potential selling price of these items, and could the lender have pressured the museum to include the collection? The museum is cultivating a major collector, hoping that the collection will be donated to the museum in the long run. As part of the courtship, the museum mounts an exhibit entirely consisting of works borrowed from this collector. The collector wants to exert considerable control over which works are displayed, and how, and what is said about them. When does this cross the boundary into exerting inappropriate levels of influence over intellectual content? (Particularly if the museum staff disagrees with the donor's choices. . . .)

VI. Financial Stability

STANDARDS REGARDING FINANCIAL STABILITY
Characteristics of Excellence Related to Financial Stability

▶ The museum legally, ethically and responsibly acquires, manages and allocates its financial resources in a way that advances its mission.

▶ The museum operates in a fiscally responsible manner that promotes its long-term sustainability.

Commentary

Short, sweet, to the point. While there are many standards from outside the museum field that impinge on this area of operations (e.g., Financial Accounting Standards Board standards, the Association of Fundraising Professionals' Code of Ethical Principles and Standards of Professional Conduct, the Panel on the Nonprofit Sector's Principles for Good Governance and Ethical Practice), museums are mostly concerned that: (1) they have enough money; (2) it was raised in a appropriate way; and (3) it is spent in accordance with the mission. There are separate standards statements dealing with what to do if there is not enough money and how to insure that the money comes from appropriate sources (with no inappropriate strings attached). See the text of these standards below.

EXECUTIVE COMPENSATION

The third point, "spent in accordance with the mission," deserves special attention. In the past decade, the press, the public and regulators have become increasingly sensitive to the issue of nonprofit executive compensation. It is a matter of some concern if the museum director's compensation is much higher than that of his or her peers, disproportionate to the museum's overall expenditures or includes perks that seem unduly lavish or unrelated to his or her duties. The press and public become particularly outraged by the perks. Actual examples from recent stories in the news include swimming pool maintenance, high-end, handmade furnishings for the director's home and first-rate travel and accommodations.

The issue of unduly high salary is more pernicious, however. More and more often, museums are engaged in major expansions, new buildings by name-brand architects, new ventures and large capital campaigns. This means there is a lot of pressure on directors to bring in big money. Some boards decide the best way to do this is to hire chief executives from the private sector, people with a background in law or financial management. Such candidates bring with them business-sector expectations regarding compensation. Also, some directors from the nonprofit sector decide that the best way to cultivate high-end donors is to adopt their lifestyle. Even if the financial equation seems clear ("if we pay this guy $x, he can bring in $y with his contacts, which is a net gain"), there is still the issue of public perception, which cannot be ignored. The public regards nonprofit museums as charities and expects museum directors to display a degree of frugality in keeping with that status. It is, after all, the public's money that is being spent, to a large extent. It behooves museums to critically examine appropriate compensation levels for their chief executives, including benchmarking themselves with their peers and with other nonprofits supported by their community.

STANDARDS REGARDING DEVELOPING AND MANAGING BUSINESS AND INDIVIDUAL DONOR SUPPORT

The reader is directed to the AAM website (www.aam-us.org) for the original, full version of this text that includes recommended procedures for documenting donor support, as well as notes regarding legal and tax compliance.

General Principles

▸ **Loyalty to mission.** To ensure accountability and informed decision making, museums should develop written policies, approved by their governing authorities, guiding the museum's development and management of business and individual support in a manner that protects their assets and reputation and is consistent with their mission.

▸ **Public trust and accountability.** The museum community recognizes and encourages appropriate collaborations with a variety of stakeholders, including a museum's donors. Such support often comes with expectations regarding involvement in the museum's activities. It is essential to a museum's public trust responsibilities that it maintain control over the content and integrity of its programs, exhibitions and activities.

▸ **Transparency.** Museums should provide business and individual donors with accurate information about mission, finances and programs.

▸ **Fidelity to donor intent.** Museums should use support from business and individual donors for purposes that are mutually agreed upon.

▸ **Ethics and conflict of interest.** In soliciting and managing business and individual support, the museum should comply with the AAM Code of Ethics for Museums and its own ethics policies, with particular attention to potential conflicts of interest.

▸ **Confidentiality.** A museum should ensure that information about donations is handled with respect for the wishes of the donor and with confidentiality to the extent provided by law.

PURPOSE AND IMPORTANCE

Not-for-profit, charitable, educational and scientific organizations and those they serve have always benefited from the business sector and the generosity of individual donors. Businesses and individual donors also have benefited from their relationships with the museum community. Through association with museums, businesses seek to positively affect their enterprise by showing their commitment to a not-for-profit's mission, generating goodwill within communities in which they operate and increasing the recognition of their business identity. Through their generosity, donors reaffirm their commitment to the arts, sciences, history and lifelong learning and to creating a stronger and more civil society by making objects and information accessible. In addition, individual donors often have family connections or other close personal relationships with the museums they support.

In light of often intricate museum-donor relationships, AAM has worked with the field to create these standards on developing and managing business and individual donor support. While these standards provide general guidance, it is essential that each museum draft its own policies appropriate to its mission and programs.

MANAGING SUPPORT

Museums should create policies regarding business and individual donor support either as separate documents or as part of other museum policies. A museum should be consistent in following its policy; any changes should be driven by evolving standards and best practices and the institution's mission and strategic direction. A museum should not change policy solely in response to a specific situation.

These policies should: identify the museum's goals for developing and managing support; define the responsibilities of the governing body and staff for decisions about business and individual donor support, including but not limited to solicitation, gift acceptance, fulfillment, recognition and public inquiry; ensure that the museum has the necessary human and financial resources for fulfilling its obligations in any donor relationship; and address conflicts of interest in situations involving business or individual donor support opportunities in which a member of the museum's governing authority or staff may have an interest.

CONFLICT OF INTEREST

The policy should address the obligation of members of the staff or governing authority to disclose any interest in the relationship under consideration. Such disclosure does not imply ethical impropriety. The museum may require that the individual recuse himself from any discussion and/or action regarding support from a business or donor with whom he or she is associated or has an interest, and document the individual's role in any other aspect of the project or program supported by that donation.

DONOR COMMUNICATION AND RELATIONSHIPS

The policy should clearly identify which staff or governing body members are authorized to make or change agreements with businesses or individual donors. In addition, a museum should have a clear policy concerning the level of financial, tax and legal information it will provide to supporters, including a policy of recommending that they consult their own legal and financial advisors.

TYPES OF SUPPORT A MUSEUM WILL ACCEPT

A museum should develop a gift acceptance policy outlining the types of support it accepts from businesses or individual donors and delineating a process for determining whether or not—from a mission, operational, business and legal perspective—to accept a gift as offered. A museum should determine whether it will exclude any business or category of business because of the business's products and services, taking into consideration the characteristics, values and attitudes of its community and audience, discipline and mission. In deciding whether to exclude certain supporters a museum may wish to consider: products and services provided by a business; the business practices of the potential supporter; and whether to associate certain exclusions with particular activities (e.g., children's programming).

RECOGNITION

A museum should consider the range of recognition it may offer a business or individual donor. In doing so, it should consider general standards for recognizing donor support based on the level of support received, such as those relating to the use, placement, size of names and signage.

CONFIDENTIALITY

A museum should ensure that a relationship of trust is established and maintained with its donors by respecting the private nature of information about the donor and the donation, if appropriate. In doing so, it may consider developing a system to control access to and handling of donor information; balancing the museum's obligation to maintain public accountability with its obligation to protect donors' privacy by outlining what type of information can and cannot be kept confidential; and collecting only relevant information about donors or potential donors.

ANONYMITY

A museum must determine whether and under what circumstances it will accept anonymous gifts. A museum should avoid agreeing to requests for anonymity that conceal a conflict of interest, real or perceived, or raise other ethical concerns.

UNCOLLECTABLE PLEDGES

Situations may arise when donors cannot or do not honor a pledge. In determining the enforceability of a pledge that is not honored, a museum may consider legal and accounting implications; the overall impact of the gift on the museum; the museum's history and previous relationship with the donor; and the attitude of the community toward the situation.

DOCUMENTATION

A museum should require that all documents relating to the development of donor support be maintained and retained in accordance with applicable law and record-retention policies.

APPLICATION OF POLICY

A museum should identify clearly all entities, such as friends groups, voluntary organizations, components of a museum system, etc., that must comply with its policies about business and individual donor support.

PUBLIC ACCOUNTABILITY

A museum should respond to all public and media inquiries about its support from businesses and individual donors, including allegations of unethical behavior, with a prompt, full and frank discussion of the issue, the institution's actions and the rationale for such actions.

ISSUES RELATED SPECIFICALLY TO BUSINESS SUPPORT

Use of Museum Names and Logos

A museum should set clear parameters for the use of any of its names and logos by a business supporter. In creating such a policy a museum might address: the contexts in which it will permit such use; its responsibility to approve all uses of its names and logos; specific prohibitions; and conformity with its policies for protecting intellectual property (e.g., trademark, copyright).

Promotion of the Museum-Business Relationship

A business may wish to promote its relationship with a museum in its marketing, advertising and public relations activities. In its policy, a museum might address: limits on the scope of how and the extent to which a business may promote its relationship with the museum, and the responsibility of the museum to approve any such promotion.

Support from Vendors

Current or potential relationships between a museum and a vendor providing goods or services should not be contingent upon a contribution from the vendor.

Exclusive Arrangements

A museum should carefully consider whether or not it is willing to enter into a relationship with a business that restricts the museum from receiving support from the business's competitors or from using a competitor's products and services.

Commentary

BALANCING EXPECTATIONS

Because most nonprofit museums are tax exempt and receive so much of their income from public sources (government funding), they are held to a high standard of conduct. And yet U.S. museums rarely have guaranteed sources of government funding, unlike their European colleagues. They are expected to aggressively pursue other sources of support, as well, including private funding. These funders—individuals or businesses—bring their own expectations to this relationship. Corporations increasingly see sponsorships as a business rather than a charitable arrangement. They want value for their money in terms of publicity and exposure. Individual donors care deeply about the museum and its mission and may be deeply vested in a project and want to be involved in key decisions regarding its execution. And while these standards specifically cite individual donors, they are equally applicable to the family foundations some of these donors have created.

These motivations are not inherently bad, they are merely human. But it is the museum's obligation to acknowledge and manage these expectations in a manner that is consistent with the public trust. A typical situation that requires careful thought occurs when museums court major collectors by mounting shows devoted to works from their collections. In some cases the press or public have questioned whether these exhibits unduly benefit the collector by increasing the value of the featured works. Some have raised the issue of whether these exhibits represent the highest curatorial judgment regarding quality and the best use of the museum's space and time. Another situation occurs when a corporate sponsor may be perceived to have an interest in the message behind an exhibit: an oil company funding an exhibit examining conservation in Alaska, for example, or a pharmaceutical company supporting an exhibit exploring traditional versus alternative medicine. The public may presume (rightly or wrongly) that the funder influenced the content. Such doubts can erode one of museums' most valued assets—our reputation for accuracy and objectivity. Application of the standards in such instances will help museums identify potential conflicts before they blossom into controversies, make appropriate decisions consistent with their policies and conventions of the field and justify their actions to the public and press in a credible manner.

DONOR INTENT

Donor intent can become a point of controversy as a museum seeks to respond sensibly to changing circumstances while honoring the original terms of a gift. At the extreme end of the spectrum are high-profile situations such as that of the Barnes Foundation in Merion, Pa. Some contend it would be truer to the intent of Albert Barnes (and his curmudgeonly resolve to snub the artistic establishment) to abolish the institution than to move it to downtown Philadelphia, even if that were the only way to ensure its survival. Such people, like strict constructionists of the U.S. Constitution, believe that donor intent is so rigid as have no flexibility, even if the proposed use seems to adhere to the spirit of the gift. Unfortunately, if the donor is dead, there is no way to ask, though sometimes family members can be approached for a proxy blessing on a reasonable alteration to the purposes for the original gift. At some point this becomes a legal issue, as the administration of such gifts is supervised by the attorney general of the state in which the museum is incorporated. But, as with so many of the issues raised in this book, the museum should grapple with the ethical dimensions of its decision before the AG becomes involved.

STANDARDS REGARDING RETRENCHMENT OR DOWNSIZING

In these challenging economic times many museums are experiencing a dramatic loss of income from multiple sources, including endowments, parent organizations, funding agencies, admissions and museum store sales. In response, many museums make changes in their governance, staffing and operations. These actions can be necessary and appropriate steps in securing the museum's future. Sometimes, however, downsizing or retrenchment is mistakenly assumed to be an indicator of bad management. This standard addresses the issues of downsizing and retrenchment, and how they may affect museums.

Downsizing and retrenchment can be responsible and necessary corrective actions in response to financial reductions. When preparing for retrenchment, museums: focus on retaining their ability to fulfill their mission and serve their community; take actions consistent with the highest ethical, fiscal and management standards in the museum field; and carefully consider the effect of their actions on their staff, their community and the collections they hold in trust for the public.

The following observations provide guidance regarding application of these standards to issues that commonly arise when a museum is considering downsizing or retrenchment.

Collections

Collections often receive special scrutiny during retrenchment either because of the expense of maintaining them appropriately or because of their potential as financial assets. In considering the role of collections in retrenchment, museums are guided by the following principles.

Collections are held in trust for the public, and a primary responsibility of the governing authority is to safeguard this trust. The museum may determine that it is unable in the long run to appropriately care for some parts of its collections. In such cases, the most responsible action may be to deaccession and transfer material to another suitable caretaker in an orderly manner that safeguards the collections and their documentation. Museums may carefully consider whether it is appropriate for the material to remain in the public domain at another nonprofit institution or whether it can responsibly be placed through public sale. Deaccessioning, however, is never a fast or simple solution. It may take a great deal of time and other resources to research the material in question, determine its provenance, identify any restrictions on the title and arrange for an appropriate and safe transfer. In the short run, it may actually require additional expenditures on the part of the museum to conduct the necessary research, prepare the documentation, arrange for disposition and affect the transfer. Deaccessioning is part of a long-term, thoughtful decision on the part of the museum about how best to fulfill its mission with available resources. It is conducted in accordance with standards and best practices in the field, and with the museum's own code of ethics, collections planning and collections policies.

Various statements of ethics in the museum field prescribe what can be done with the funds resulting from deaccessioning. All museums are expected to abide by the AAM Code of Ethics for Museums and by any additional codes of ethics particular to their discipline. The AAM Code of Ethics for Museums specifies that proceeds from sales resulting from deaccessioning can be used only for acquisitions or direct care of collections. While the interpretation of "direct care" varies between museums and disciplines, there is a strong consensus that it does not include use of funds to pay operational expenses. The code of ethics of the Association of Art Museum Directors (AAMD) explicitly specifies that art museums can only use funds resulting from deaccessioning for the acquisition of new collections, and that of the American Association of State and Local History (AASLH) specifies that history museums can use such funds only for acquisition or preservation.

There is increasing pressure on museums to capitalize their collections and to use them as collateral for financial loans to the museum. The AAM Code of Ethics for Museums requires that collections be "unencumbered," which means that collections cannot be used as collateral for a loan. The AAMD code of ethics also precludes using collections as collateral, and further bars museums from capitalizing collections. The AASLH has also issued a position statement that declares that capitalizing collections is unethical.

A museum's collections are valuable only insofar as they are accessible to the public and to scholars and the information inherent in them is preserved through documentation and the knowledge of those who care for them. "Mothballing" collections, i.e., putting them in storage and eliminating or minimizing curation and use, may seem a desirable short-term strategy for cost reductions, but it carries measurable risks. Many kinds of collections are not stable in storage without constant monitoring and attention. Often, collections can be made accessible in a meaningful way only through the mediation of an experienced, knowledgeable staff that, once dismantled, may not easily be rebuilt.

Human Resources

Museums often reduce staff size in response to financial reductions. This may be accomplished by leaving positions temporarily unfilled, eliminating individual positions or eliminating whole departments or program areas. In considering the reduction of staff as a part of retrenchment, museums consider the short-term and long-term needs of the institution. Leaving a position vacant when a staff member departs is less traumatic than laying off existing staff. It can also, however, leave key positions and vital roles unfilled at a crucial time. Museums weigh the needs of the staff and the needs of the institution in choosing a strategy for staff reductions.

Museums also consider the impact of downsizing on the museum's programs and operations. The museum's mission is accomplished primarily through its staff, but many museums also rely on volunteers and partnerships with other institutions. Staff reductions are planned in light of the overall impact on the museum's mission and activities and as part of an overall strategy for scaling back operations, supplementing paid staff with volunteers or partnerships or other strategies for accomplishing the museum's goals.

MUSEUMS IN NON-MUSEUM PARENT ORGANIZATIONS

Museums that are part of a college or university or organized under municipal, county or state government have additional factors that affect their response to a financial crisis. When parent organizations need to make financial cuts, the museum may bear a disproportionate portion of the burden. Many museums within larger parent organizations have increased their financial stability by cultivating diverse sources of income. This is particularly important to museums in parent organizations. Museums that derive significant portions of their income from outside sources are less dependent on funding from their parent organizations. This minimizes the impact of funding cuts from the parent and the likelihood that the parent will see eliminating the museum as an attractive financial strategy.

Museums can also develop a separately incorporated friends organization. A separate 501(c)3 support group can provide significant income, serve as an advocate for the museum and buffer it against sudden organizational changes. A formal memorandum of agreement between the parent and the friends group can ensure that the support organization has a voice in any decisions concerning the museum's future.

Another strategy is to embed the museum in the parent organization's operations. A museum that is an integral part of its parent organization is less likely to be an immediate target for financial reductions by the parent. By being strongly connected to the community served by the parent, reaching out to a broad constituency, attracting new sources of funding, garnering positive publicity and, most of all, being valued by a large number of people, a museum makes itself less vulnerable to cutbacks. An active and engaged constituency will encourage the parent organization to continue its support.

Parent organizations usually have no legal obligation to continue to operate a museum. They may not consider the possibility that the museum can lose accreditation as a result of changes made as part of retrenchment. AAM, representing the public's interest of stewardship of collections held in the public domain, urges parent organizations to take into account the following moral, ethical and practical issues. First, museums are a part of an institution's long-term strategy of civic engagement. Any decisions regarding the future of museums operated by a parent organization should take into account their long-term role in serving the broader public good. While in the short run, cutbacks to a museum may result in financial savings, in the long run they may damage the parent organization's ability to serve its community and reach out to a broad audience. And second, museums operate in the public interest and hold their collections as a public trust. If a parent organization is considering downsizing or closing a museum, it has an ethical obligation to do so in a manner that safeguards the public's interest. The fate of the collections must be carefully considered. Having taken on the obligation of caring for collections, the parent must plan to transfer this stewardship to another suitable caretaker in an orderly manner that safeguards the collections and their documentation. The new caretaker should be carefully chosen with attention to its ability to care for the collections and to continue to provide public and scholarly access. As discussed earlier in this standard, this process may require additional resources in the short term and may not be a useful strategy for immediate cost savings.

VII. Facilities and Risk Management

STANDARDS REGARDING FACILITIES AND RISK MANAGEMENT
Characteristics of Excellence Related to Facilities and Risk Management

▶ The museum is a good steward of its resources held in the public trust.

▶ The museum demonstrates a commitment to providing the public with physical and intellectual access to the museum and its resources.

▶ The museum complies with local, state and federal laws, codes and regulations applicable to its facilities, operations and administration.

▶ The museum allocates its space and uses its facilities to meet the needs of the collections, audience and staff.

▶ The museum has appropriate measures to ensure the safety and security of people, its collections and objects and the facilities it owns or uses.

▶ The museum has an effective program for the care and long-term maintenance of its facilities.

▶ The museum is clean, well maintained and provides for visitors' needs.

▶ The museum takes appropriate measures to protect itself against potential risk and loss.

PURPOSE AND IMPORTANCE
Museums care for their resources in trust for the public. It is incumbent upon them to ensure the safety of their staff, visitors and neighbors, maintain their buildings and grounds, and minimize risk to the collections that they preserve for future generations. Conscious, proactive identification of the risks that could potentially harm people and collections, and appropriate allocation of resources to reduce these risks are vital to museum management.

IMPLEMENTATION
Simply put, a museum should manage its facilities, e.g., buildings and grounds, in such a manner as to ensure that they are clean, well maintained, safe and accessible.

Risk management is an institution-wide activity encompassing functions as diverse as building and site security, visitor services, integrated pest management, storage and use of hazardous materials, and insurance. A museum should manage risk to ensure: that risks to people (visitors, staff, neighbors) and to collections are accurately identified and assessed; that appropriate methods are employed to avoid, block, mitigate, share and assume or insure against risk; and that resources are appropriately allocated so as to have the greatest effect on reducing risk to people, facilities and collections.

Museums should also have regular, adequate training of staff in implementing an emergency-preparedness plan, including practice or drills; inspections related to facilities and risk (fire, health and safety, etc., as appropriate to the institution's circumstances); a process for addressing deficiencies identified in these inspections; and a program of health and safety training for staff and volunteers, as appropriate to the institution's circumstances. Museums are expected to comply with all applicable local, state and federal laws, codes and regulations.

STANDARDS FOR FACILITIES AND RISK MANAGEMENT AS RELATED TO CONTRACTORS

When museums contract key services related to facilities (e.g., food service, museum store, housekeeping, security), they are expected to require contractors to abide by national standards regarding facilities and risk management. If the museum does not have control over the contract governing this relationship (e.g., a city hires and supervises contractors operating in the museum's building), the museum should educate contractors on national standards and encourage them to abide by them.

STANDARDS FOR MUSEUMS HOUSED IN HISTORIC STRUCTURES

Museums housed in historic structures should balance the preservation needs of the building with actions necessary to mitigate risk to people and to the collections housed in the building. The standards do not dictate specifically how this is achieved; they focus instead on the outcome of appropriate risk management. For example, a historic house museum needs to weigh all relevant factors (mission, resources, impact on the structure, alternative mitigation techniques) when deciding whether to install an automated fire suppression system. In order to be accountable, the institution should be able to explain how its decisions are appropriate to its circumstances.

DOCUMENTATION

Museums should have a current, comprehensive emergency/disaster-preparedness plan that is tailored to the institution's needs and specific circumstances; covers all relevant threats; addresses staff, visitors, structures and collections; includes evacuation plans for people; specifies how to protect, evacuate or recover collections in the event of a disaster; and delegates responsibility for implementation. Museums should also have certificates of inspection related to facilities and risk, as appropriate to their circumstances, when such certificates are provided by the inspecting agency.

Commentary

EMERGENCY PREPAREDNESS

Recent research by Heritage Preservation revealed the appalling state of emergency-preparedness planning in the United States. Only 20 percent of museums have an emergency-preparedness plan that covers collections and staff trained to implement it. Yet such plans are essential to museums fulfilling their roles as good stewards of the cultural, artistic, historic and scientific resources they hold in trust for the public. As a museum works toward meeting national standards, AAM strongly urges that it prioritize the development of an emergency-preparedness plan and training of staff in implementation.

INSURANCE

Museums frequently ask whether museum standards require them to carry insurance on their collections. The answer is no, they don't. What they do mandate is a well-considered, balanced approach to risk management that provides appropriate protection overall for people, facilities and collections. For most museums, some level of collections insurance is one element in this approach. Even if the collections are unique and in that sense irreplaceable in the event of a loss, insurance enables the museum to acquire new collections that provide some comparable benefit to its audience. It is far preferable, however, to prevent such a loss to begin with, and in allocating resources the museum should carefully examine how to balance prevention and mitigation (human and automated security systems, climate control, fire suppression, conservation) with insurance.

SECTION 3
COMPLETING THE PICTURE

The Universe of Museum Standards and Best Practices
WHEN ARE OTHER STANDARDS APPLICABLE TO YOUR MUSEUM?

There are many, many standards promulgated by groups large and small, inside and outside the museum field, which may influence museums. The most prominent of these are discussed below. Museums may come across or be presented with standards, however, from a variety of sources. It may help to examine the following criteria in deciding whether these standards are appropriate guides for your museum's policies and procedures.

Are the standards in question formally adopted or endorsed by at least one nonprofit organization that is broadly representative of the field, or of the segment of the field to which the standards apply? Are they broadly applicable to museums of all types and sizes? Or if only applicable to particular segments of the museum field (e.g., discipline-specific standards), then are they broadly applicable to all museums of that segment? Are they nonprescriptive—describing desirable outcomes, rather than endorsing particular methods of achieving those outcomes? Are they based, when possible, on applicable existing, widely accepted principles and practices in the field? Have they been developed through a broadly inclusive process that gathers input from museums of relevant disciplines, geographic location, size, governance type and other relevant variables? Have they been reviewed through a broadly inclusive process that invites, formally reviews and incorporates input? Are they restricted to areas of practice for which there exists broad consensus in the field? And finally, are they consonant with sound management of the museum as a whole?

Consider these questions, assess whether your museum is represented by the group promulgating the standards and decide whether it is appropriate for you to adopt them as voluntary standards. A general museum, for example, that includes both history and natural history collections should consider whether it will abide by both the American Association for State and Local History's standards and those of the Society for the Preservation of Natural History Collections. An art museum that has not been invited to participate in the Association of Art Museum Directors should consider whether it will abide by these standards even though they have been developed with the input of only a segment of the field.

It is very important to discuss these options in advance of any actual decision that would be influenced by the standards, as the looming real-world consequences of such decisions can have unfortunate effects on people's judgment. Also, creating or revising policies while a controversial decision is in play can lead the public to question the integrity of the process.

Other Major Sources of Standards Relevant to Museums

The following is a list of other major sources of standards relevant to museums and the most prominent of the policy documents they present to the field. Consult the AAM website for a more extensive list and for links to these documents.

MUSEUM-RELATED PROFESSIONAL ASSOCIATIONS (DISCIPLINE OR FUNCTION SPECIFIC, REGIONAL)

American Association for State and Local History (AASLH)
▶ Statement of Professional Standards and Ethics
▶ Ethics Position Paper #1: Capitalization of Collections
▶ Ethics Position Paper #2: When a History Museum Closes

American Institute for Conservation of Historic and Artistic Works
▶ Code of Ethics and Guidelines for Practice

American Public Gardens Association
▶ Voluntary Code of Conduct for Botanic Gardens and Arboreta
▶ Code Regarding Invasive Plant Species

Association of Art Museum Directors (AAMD)
▶ Professional Practices in Art Museums
▶ Report on Sacred Objects
▶ Report on Incoming Loans of Archaeological Material and Ancient Art
▶ Report of the AAMD Task Force on Collecting
▶ Report of the AAMD Task Force on Nazi Looted Art, Addendum

Association of Children's Museums
▶ ACM Standards Document **Association of Railway Museums**
▶ Recommended Practices for Railway Museums

Association of Science-Technology Centers
▶ Accessible Practices

Association of Zoos and Aquariums
▶ Code of Professional Ethics

International Council of Museums
▶ ICOM: Code of Ethics for Museums

International Committee for Documentation (CIDOC) of the International Council of Museums (ICOM)
- ◗ International Guidelines for Museum Object Information

Midwest Open Air Museums Coordinating Council
- ◗ Statement of Professional Conduct

Museum Store Association
- ◗ Code of Ethics
- ◗ Ethics Policies for Archaeological and Ethnological Resources
- ◗ Ethics Policies for Endangered Natural Heritage

National Initiative for a Networked Cultural Heritage and the Humanities
- ◗ Guide to Good Practice in the Digital Representation and Management of Cultural Heritage Materials

National Park Service's Northeast Region
- ◗ NPS: Guidelines for the Treatment of Historic Furnished Interiors in Accordance with the Secretary of the Interior's Standards for the Treatment of Historic Properties

The Secretary of the Interior
- ◗ Standards for the Treatment of Historic Properties Includes Standards for Preservation, Rehabilitation, Restoration and Reconstruction

Society for the Preservation of Natural History Collections
- ◗ Guidelines for the Care of Natural History Collections

Southeastern College Art Conference
- ◗ Guidelines for College and University Museums and Galleries

Tri-State Coalition for Historic Places
- ◗ Standards and Practices for Historic Site Administration

ASSOCIATIONS REPRESENTING THE BROADER NONPROFIT OR ACADEMIC SECTOR

American Historical Association
- ◗ Standards for Museum Exhibits Dealing with Historical Objects
- ◗ Statement on Standards of Professional Conduct

Association of Fundraising Professionals
- ◗ Code of Ethical Principles and Standards of Professional Practice
- ◗ The Accountable Nonprofit Organization

BBB Wise Giving Alliance
- ◗ Standards of Charitable Accountability

College Art Association
- Guidelines Concerning Part-Time Professional Employment
- Guidelines Adopted by CAA Regarding the Hiring by Museums of Guest Curators, Exhibitors/Artists and Catalogue Essayists as Outside Contractors
- Professional Practices for Art Museum Curators
- Resolution Concerning the Acquisition of Cultural Properties Originating in Foreign Countries
- Resolution Concerning the Sale and Exchange of Works of Art by Museums

Independent Sector
- Principles for Good Governance and Ethical Practice: A Guideline for Charities and Foundations

National Council on Public History
- NCPH: Ethics Guidelines

AAM Standing Professional Committees and Standards

AAM currently has 13 Standing Professional Committees representing professional segments of the field (registrars, curators, security, educators, managers, public relations and marketing staff, evaluators, media and technology staff, exhibit designers, development and membership) as well as small museums, professionals involved in museum training programs and people concerned about the issue of staff diversity. Many of these committees have developed standards or best practice statements related to the areas of museum operation that fall within their purview. As of this writing, these standards have not yet been reviewed and approved as national standards and best practices by the AAM board, Accreditation Commission and Council of Standing Professional Committees. For this reason, they are not yet endorsed by AAM as an association. However, they represent the best thinking of professionals in these fields of endeavor on the issues faced in their work. As they are reviewed, revised and approved by AAM's governance, they will be posted to the AAM website and added to future editions of this book.

The major documents promulgated by the Standing Professional Committees are:
Code of Ethics for Registrars, developed by the Registrars Committee (RCAAM)
Code of Ethics, 1991, developed by the Development and Membership Standing Professional Committee (DAM)
Code of Practice for Couriering Museum Objects, developed by the Registrars Committee (RCAAM)
Curators Code of Ethics, 1996, developed by the Curators' Committee (CurCom)
Professional Standards for the Practice of Audience Research and Evaluation in Museums, developed by the Committee on Audience Research and Evaluation (CARE)

Standards and Best Practice in Museum Education, developed by the Committee on
    Education (EdCom)

Standards for Museum Exhibitions and Indicators of Excellence, developed by the
    Standing Professional Committees Council

Suggested Guidelines in Museum Security, developed by the Museum Association
    Security Committee in collaboration with the Museum, Library and Cultural
    Properties Council of American Society for Industrial Security International

Trends and Potential Future Standards

We can't foresee the future, but we can make some pretty good guesses based on monitoring discussions among the museum field, coverage by the press, legislative efforts by
regulators and expectations of funders. Based on these observations, it is likely that the
following trends will influence standards in the coming years.

TRANSPARENCY AND ACCOUNTABILITY

Policymakers at the state and federal level will continue to raise the bar for nonprofit
accountability. If nothing else, as long as Sen. Charles Grassley (R-Iowa) continues to be
re-elected, nonprofits in general, and some museums in particular, will continue to receive
close scrutiny. In order to avoid inappropriate or overly prescriptive legislative mandates
governing our behavior, museums will need to develop more stringent voluntary standards
regarding reporting their own financial and programmatic performance as well as compensation of directors and board members. Groups like BBB-Wise Giving, Charity Navigator
and GuideStar are encouraging private donors to require a good deal of performance
information from museums before handing over their funds. If museums don't develop
voluntary standards for what they report to the public and how, it is likely to be imposed
upon us.

    What you can do to be prepared: Think about what the public, press, policymakers
and funders want to know about your museum, and what you want them to know. Start
designing ways to make this information available. The World Wide Web is a fabulous
medium for sharing information at relatively low cost. Documents you might want
to share broadly include your mission statement, institutional plan, audited financial
statements, IRS 990 reporting form and key policy documents (ethics, collections management, etc.). Think about designing your own measure of success—a score sheet, as
it were—to shape how your constituents assess your progress. Basic information might
include simple "outputs" (counts) of attendance, acquisitions, number of exhibits, programs and publications. It is even more powerful to report on results (outcomes) based
on evaluation data. How did your major new exhibit change the knowledge, beliefs and
attitudes of visitors? How has your high school internship program affected the career
choice of participants? Did your marketing partnership with local merchants help direct

visitor spending into the local economy? Taking charge of how such information is compiled and shared both demonstrates appropriate stewardship of public resources and ensures that you maintain control of your museum's image.

PLANNING, PLANNING AND YET MORE PLANNING

You may have noticed the recurring phrase in the Standards in Translation that reiterates that museums should "decide what they are going to do... and put it in writing." Grant makers and philanthropic foundations are increasingly concerned that recipients of their funding demonstrate that they know what they are going to do with the funds, and that their plan is part of an integrated, sustainable vision for the museum. The Institute of Museum and Library Services used to give general operating support—but that time is gone forever. The Government Performance and Results Act (GPRA) sounded the death knell for that era in the realm of federal grants when it became law in 1993. Federal granting agencies need to be able to demonstrate what, precisely, the public's money is being used to accomplish. Private foundations are increasingly adopting the same approach.

What you can do to be prepared: Planning isn't rocket science; it doesn't have to require expensive consultants or massive amounts of staff time. A small museum can make planning part of the institutional culture by starting to write things down as decisions are made, and ensure these written versions are approved by the board and shared with everyone. No elaborate template is necessary—just start simple and build from there. A bigger museum with more complex operations can devote more resources to formal planning, and probably needs to. The larger the staff and budget and the more projects the museum is engaged in at one time (exhibits, programs, publications, research, fundraising), the more important it is that these activities be integrated, prioritized and understood by all involved. The time you put into planning will be repaid by the increased effectiveness of your activities and increased ability to raise support to make the plans a reality.

EVALUATION

At the other end of the pipeline, both government and private funders increasingly expect formal evaluation data to demonstrate that the plan actually worked and had measurable effects (whether the evaluation addresses the knowledge and attitude of visitors or the economic health of the community). Frankly, there is already strong consensus in the museum field that evaluation is necessary and desirable. The only thing that has kept it from being codified in national standards is the fact that so many museums, even accredited ones, would immediately flunk the standard. This is evidently a very difficult thing to do well (even at large museums with a lot of resources), but the day is coming when museums are going to have to figure it out.

What you can do to be prepared: Evaluation isn't rocket science, either, but it may be chemistry lab—a little more complex and harder to master than planning, judging from the progress (or lack thereof) of the field in adopting it. Take small steps first. Think about the desired outcomes of any given project or activity and decide, at least conceptually, how you would measure whether it was successful. Identify your most important projects and activities, and start implementing an evaluation program for these areas of operations. Include at least a small line item for evaluation in the budgets for these projects and activities, identify who on staff is responsible for designing and conducting the evaluation and make sure the results are actually shared and used to make decisions. Help is often available from local colleges or universities. Find out whether students in related fields of study are required to do individual or class projects and enlist their aid. Use free online project evaluation resources such as that available from the Institute of Museum and Library Services.

GREEN DESIGN

There is increasing pressure from within and outside the field for museums to take greater responsibility for the health of our environment by adopting eco-friendly principles for operation and design. There is not any national standard regarding "green" design at this time, but it will be an item for discussion by the field in the coming decade.

What you can do to be prepared: Discuss with the board and staff whether they value and feel the museum ought to adopt ecologically conscious business practices. Are such practices related to your mission? Even if the answer is "no," do people feel that these practices are in alignment with your values as a business and with the expectations of your community? If so, then start considering ecological impact as one aspect of decision making and start identifying small steps that can make a difference. First steps can be as simple as providing recycling bins in public and staff areas, using recycled materials for office and program supplies, supporting low-impact commuting (car pools, public transport, bicycling) among staff in tangible ways and using low-energy appliances and office equipment. As opportunities for larger impact arise (renovations, a new building project, upgrades to building systems), factor green design into your decision making and budgeting. Some museums are designing buildings to Leadership in Energy and Environmental Design (LEED) standards, either with or without formal certification.

COLLECTIONS PLANNING

There is not yet an expectation that each museum have a collections plan, but it is highly likely that in the near future this will become a document required by national standards—and will be as fundamental as an institutional plan or a code of ethics. (See the discussion of this issue under Collections Stewardship.)

What you can do to be prepared: Consider starting collections planning in advance of it becoming a standard. A collections plan can help your museum build a shared vision for the collections, set priorities for acquisitions and improvements to care, and convince collectors to donate specific material or funders to support collections care needs. Even if you feel you already have this vision, having it in writing and formally approved by the governing authority helps you make a compelling case for support. It can give the museum the energy boost it needs to tackle necessary, appropriate (but usually not enjoyable) deaccessioning. And you may well find that when you bring staff, board members and external constituents into the planning discussion, there is not as much of a shared vision as you thought.

CULTURAL/BIOLOGICAL/INTELLECTUAL PROPERTY ISSUES

If you follow the news at all, you are aware of the heightened international concern regarding ownership and repatriation of cultural property. Recently Italy, Greece and Peru have all aggressively pursued claims against museums for material that they feel was acquired, exported or retained in contravention of the laws of its country of origin. The legal aspects of this fall outside the scope of our discussion. Of course museums are expected to abide by the law, though with cultural property questions, picking your way through the morass of national and international laws and treaties is itself a challenge. The ethical aspects, however, are very much our business and will affect how the legal aspects play out, both in terms of the potential for new treaties or regulations and in how foreign governments (or the U.S. government) choose to pursue legal claims. The museum field is currently grappling with the ethical dimensions of acquisitions and claims regarding antiquities and archaeological materials. Soon there will be national and discipline-specific standards and best practices guiding museum conduct in these areas. The next frontiers will be biological material (e.g., genetic prospecting, ethnobotany, paleontological specimens) and intellectual property (e.g., cultural knowledge regarding traditional medicine and ownership/intellectual control of songs, stories, religious and cultural ceremonies).

What you can do to be prepared: Start by reviewing your internal standards for documentation of acquisitions. Do you require staff to aggressively check documentation to uncover potential problems, or is it sufficient that the donor or seller provide assurances? Identify all areas of your operations (collecting, research, loans, exhibits, publications) that potentially trigger concerns in any of the areas mentioned above. Being aware of the ethical dimensions of these activities and the concerns of source countries or native cultures enables you to begin creating your own policies regarding appropriate behavior. This, in turn, will shape the field's dialogues on these issues and help us to develop appropriate national standards to guide museums and provide support for their decisions.

Troubleshooting

PROBLEMS . . .

When the public, press or policymakers don't like the way an individual museum or museums in general are behaving, they have a number of very effective ways to apply pressure. Members of the public can withhold their support in the form of attendance, donations or their vote on local initiatives important to the museum, such as bond levies or easements. They can write letters to the press and to representatives at the local, state and federal levels of government. They can also ask the attorney general of their state to take action if they feel a legal abuse of the museum's obligations as a servant in the public trust has occurred.

The press can do an extremely effective job of spreading bad news, whatever it is, catching the attention of the public and policymakers. News outlets may or may not fairly represent your position in the matter, and they may or may not accurately present the facts. But one big story can expose more people to your museum than any single piece of PR you have paid for—without your having control over the message.

Policymakers can withhold funds at the state or local level (or at least they can try). Most importantly for the field as a whole, they may take away the freedom of museums to self-regulate if they feel that our self-imposed standards are insufficient or that our voluntary compliance is ineffective.

For all these reasons, it is extremely important that museums consider what can go wrong and how to deal with it when creating and applying policies that guide their operations. The issues that most often attract the attention of policymakers, press and the public are (though not necessarily in rank order):

▶ Deaccessioning of collections items

▶ Use of funds resulting from the sale of deaccessioning collections

▶ Executive compensation

▶ Changes to the exterior of the museum that affect local quality of life issues (e.g., parking lots, landscaping, renovations to the building that change its footprint or height)

▶ Changes to museum operations that affect local quality of life issues (e.g., increasing attendance or frequency of special events, thus affecting local traffic, parking, noise, etc.)

▶ Controversial exhibit content (with particular hot buttons being religion and pornography, and especially anything that combines the two)

▶ Operating in a manner that benefits an individual or private company

▶ Conflicts of interest on the parts of staff or members of the governing authority

The good news is that by writing and following policies based on nationally recognized standards, a museum can go a long way toward defending its actions and defusing potentially damaging situations. The bad news is that once the problem has blown up, it is usually too late to go back and consult the standards to fix things. Here is a brief guide on how to use the standards presented in this book, and other applicable standards, to guide your decision making and shape your response to concerned constituents.

. . . AND HOW TO AVOID THEM

1. Create policies ahead of time. Policies prepared during a crisis or after controversial actions, retroactively validating the museum's decision, lack credibility.

2. When drafting the policies, involve a diverse group that can look at the issue from a variety of perspectives and help foresee potential concerns from various constituencies.

3. Base policies on nationally recognized standards in the museum and related nonprofit fields. Document your reasoning regarding the standards you choose to adopt and (more importantly) those you choose not to adopt. This is particularly important if you consciously choose to adopt a policy that is in conflict with national standards in some regard. Be prepared to make a clear and compelling case for the reasoning behind your choice.

4. Ensure that policies are formally approved by the museum's governing authority and marked with the date of approval.

5. Review key policies in the introductory training given to all staff and members of the governing authority, and make sure all policies are readily accessible to staff and board.

6. When making a decision that bears on museum standards and is potentially controversial, start thinking about your communications plan right away. Designate who will be empowered to speak on the museum's behalf (making sure everyone else knows they are not authorized to do so) and ensure that they are well briefed on their message.

7. When making the decision, start by reviewing the museum's policies and the relevant standards and best-practice statements, as well as the museum's mission, vision statement (if you have one) and institutional and other relevant plans. You should be able to demonstrate that the decision aligns with all these documents.

8. The staff and board of museums are only human. No one can reasonably expect their decisions to be perfect, but you should be able to demonstrate that they are judicious, well informed, well intentioned and grounded in an understanding of the legal and ethical issues involved.

9. Consider whether and how you want to proactively communicate the decision. Especially with an inherently controversial decision, breaking the story yourself can help you control the message and avoid any appearance of secrecy.

APPENDIX

Dates of Approval of Standards and Best Practices

The following list provides the original title and dates of initial approval/revision for each standard or best practice statement included in this book. As a group, these documents were approved as "Standards and Best Practices for U.S. Museums" by the AAM Board of Directors in November 2006.

Characteristics of Excellence (Characteristics of an Accreditable Museum. Approved 1996, revised 2005.)

AAM Standards Regarding Institutional Mission Statements (The Accreditation Commission's Expectations Regarding Institutional Mission Statements. Approved 1999, revised 2004.)

AAM Standards Regarding Institutional Planning (The Accreditation Commission's Expectations Regarding Institutional Planning. Approved 1999, revised 2004.)

The AAM Code of Ethics for Museums (Museum Ethics: A report to the American Association of Museums, 1978. AAM Code of Ethics for Museums, approved 1993.)

AAM Standards Regarding Institutional Codes of Ethics (The Accreditation Commission's Expectations Regarding an Institutional Codes of Ethics. Approved 1999, revised 2004.)

AAM Standards Regarding Governance (The Accreditation Commission's Expectations Regarding Governance. Approved 2004.)

AAM Standards Regarding Delegation of Authority (The Accreditation Commission's Expectations Regarding Delegation of Authority. Approved 2000, revised 2004.)

AAM Standards Regarding Collections Stewardship (The Accreditation Commission's Expectations Regarding Collections Stewardship. Approved 2001, revised 2004.)

AAM Standards Regarding the Unlawful Appropriation of Objects During the Nazi Era (Guidelines Regarding the Unlawful Appropriation of Objects During the Nazi Era. Approved 1999, revised 2001.)

AAM Best Practices Regarding Loaning Collections to Non-Museum Entities (Accreditation Commission Statement Regarding Best Practices: Loaning Collections to Non-Museum Entities. Approved 2006.)

AAM Standards Regarding Exhibiting Borrowed Objects (Guidelines on Exhibiting Borrowed Objects. Approved 2000.)

AAM Standards Regarding Developing and Managing Business and Individual Donor Support (Guidelines for Museums on Developing and Managing Business Support. Approved 2001. Guidelines for Museums on Developing and Managing Individual Donor Support. Approved 2002.)

AAM Standards Regarding Retrenchment or Downsizing (Considerations for AAM Accredited Museums Facing Retrenchment or Downsizing. Approved 2003.)

AAM Standards Regarding Facilities and Risk Management (Approved 2007.)

GLOSSARY

Accessioning: (a) Formal act of accepting an object(s) into the category of materials that a museum holds in the public trust; (b) the creation of an immediate, brief and permanent record utilizing a control number for an object or group of objects added to the collection from the same source at the same time, and for which the museum has custody, right or title. Customarily, an accession record includes, among other data, the accession number; the date and nature of acquisition (gift, excavation, expedition, purchase, bequest, etc.); the source; a brief identification and description; condition; provenance; value; and name of staff member recording the accession.

Benchmark: A point of reference used in measuring and judging quality or value.

Benchmarking: The process of comparing your museum's operations to some point of reference for the purpose of setting goals, evaluating performance and making decisions about whether and how to change. There are three points of reference: internal comparison between departments or against the museum's history, external comparison to selected peers and external comparison to the museum field.

Business support: Any support, financial or in-kind, that is philanthropic or driven by marketing, advertising or public relations provided by a business (corporation, partnership, agency, family business, etc.), regardless of the nature and value of the benefit provided by a museum, or the tax implications of the relationship.

Bylaws: Legal documents that describe matters delegated to the governing authority, such as membership categories, the logistics of scheduling and holding meetings of the corporation and the governing authority, committee charges and provisions for amendments. Self-regulatory provisions for the governing authority, such as membership in the organization, attendance requirements and termination, also are in the bylaws.

Care: The museum keeps appropriate and adequate records pertaining to the provenance, identification and location of the museum's holdings and applies current, professionally accepted methods to their security and the minimization of damage and deterioration.

Collections: Objects, living or nonliving, that museums hold in trust for the public. Items usually are considered part of the museum's collections once they are accessioned. Some museums designate different categories of collections (permanent, research, educational) that functionally receive different types of care or use. These categories and their ramifications are established in the museum's collections management policy.

Collections management policy: A written document approved by the governing authority that specifies the museum's policies concerning all collections-related issues, including accessioning, documentation, storage and disposition. Policies are general guidelines that regulate the activities of the organization. They provide standards for exercising good judgment.

Collections plan: A plan that guides the content of the collections and leads staff in a coordinated and uniform direction over time to refine and expand the value of the collections in a predetermined way. Plans are time-limited and identify specific goals to be achieved. They also provide a rationale for those choices and specify how they will be achieved, who will implement the plan, when it will happen and what it will cost.

Community: Each museum self-identifies the community or communities it serves. This may be a geographically defined community (e.g., neighborhood, academic campus, town, city, county or region), a community of interest (e.g., the scientific community, the international business community), a group viewed as forming a distinct segment of society (e.g., the gay community, the Asian community) or a combination of these types.

Deaccessioning: Formal process of removing an accessioned object or group of objects from the museum's collections. A museum still owns a deaccessioned object until it disposes of it but no longer holds it in the public trust. Removing the object from the museum's possession is commonly referred to as *disposal*.

Director: The individual who is delegated authority for the day-to-day operations of the museum and allocated resources sufficient to operate the museum effectively. Functionally, this position is the chief executive officer with responsibilities including, but not limited to, hiring and firing staff, executing the budget, implementing policies and managing programs and staff. May be called CEO, museum administrator, site manager, curator, etc.

Emergency/disaster-preparedness plan: Written policies and procedures intended to prevent or minimize damage to people (staff and visitors), buildings, collections, archival materials or organizational records resulting from natural and man-made events that threaten the building and the people and objects inside it. All museums are expected to have plans that address how the museum will care for staff, visitors and collections in case of emergency. This includes evacuation plans for staff and visitors, and plans for how to protect, evacuate or recover collections in the event of disaster.

Fiduciary: Of or relating to a holding of something in trust for another: a fiduciary heir; a fiduciary contract; of or being a trustee or trusteeship; held in trust.

Governance manual: Reference manual assembled for use by members of the governing authority to assist with orientation, training and ongoing work. It may include, for example, copies of the museum's mission statement, bylaws, current institutional plan, policies and minutes of past meetings.

Governing authority: The body with legal and fiduciary responsibility for a museum. Unless delegated to another body or through a chain of command, also responsible for approving museum policy. Names of the governing authority include but are not limited to: board of commissioners, board of directors, board of managers, board of regents, board of trustees, city council, commission.

Health and safety training: Theoretical and practical instruction regarding such issues as office ergonomics, safe lifting, blood-borne and airborne pathogen safety, hazards communication and use of material safety data sheets.

Individual donor support: Cash, real property or planned gifts from an individual, family or family foundation, regardless of the use of the support or the tax implications of the gift. For the purposes of these standards, individual donor support does not include donations of collections.

Inspections related to facilities and risk: May include, for example, building occupancy permits, fire department inspections, health inspections of food service operations, USDA inspections of animal displays and insurer inspections for safety issues.

Institutional plan: Comprehensive plan that broadly delineates where the institution is going and provides sufficient detail to guide implementation. Sets priorities and guides important decisions that are oriented toward the future. Some museums split this into two parts: (1) multiyear plan: a "big picture" plan that sets strategies, goals and priorities and is sometimes referred to as a strategic or long-range plan; and (2) operational plan: a plan that provides the details needed to implement the decisions in the strategic or long-range plan. This usually focuses on a short period of time, typically geared toward the museum's budget year. Sometimes referred to as an implementation plan. There is great variability in how museums refer to these planning documents or divide particular functions between them. AAM does not mandate a particular format or nomenclature.

Integrated pest management (IPM): The coordination of information about pests and environmental conditions with available pest control methods to prevent unacceptable levels of pest damage while minimizing hazards to people, property, collections and the environment. IPM programs apply a holistic approach to pest management decision making and consider all appropriate options, including but not limited to pesticides.

Joint governance: A governance structure in which two or more entities share governance of a museum. This involves dividing or sharing basic governance responsibilities such as determining mission and purpose; hiring, supporting and evaluating the director; strategic planning; obtaining and managing resources; and monitoring the organization's programs and services. For example, this could be a museum jointly governed by a city government, which owns the collections and the building and employs the staff, and a private nonprofit, which determines museum policy and operates the museum. Or it could be a university that owns and manages a museum but delegates responsibility for determining programs and services to an advisory board. Joint governance does not automatically include museums that have separately incorporated friends organizations, unless the friends organization has significant responsibility for governance of the museum delegated to it in writing.

Objects: Materials used to communicate and motivate learning and instruments for carrying out the museum's stated purpose.

Remote governance: Governance in which the museum director reports only indirectly, through a chain of command, to the actual governing authority. For example: The governing authority of a university museum might be the board of regents, and the director reports through the provost, to the university president, to the regents. The director of a museum in the state parks department might report through a parks manager, to the head of the state department of parks and recreation, to the governor.

Risk management: The overall process of identifying, controlling and minimizing the impact of uncertain events in order to reduce the likelihood of their occurrence or the severity of their impact.

Supporting group: A group whose primary purpose is to support the museum but that has no governing authority or responsibility for the museum. The group may provide financial support, volunteers, expertise or advocacy to complement the knowledge and skills of the governing authority. Supporting groups may be called, for example, advisory boards, friends, guilds or auxiliary boards.

▶ Internal supporting groups are part of the museum itself, either as an informal association or by appointment of the governing authority. They serve at the pleasure and under the direction of the museum's governing authority or its designee.

▶ External supporting groups are informal associations or separately incorporated nonprofit entities. They are independent of the museum in their own governance. AAM expects there to be a letter of understanding, a management agreement or other document detailing the relationship between an external supporting group and the museum's governing authority.